ATROPOS PRESS
new york • dresden

Can Computers Create Art?

James Morris

Think Media EGS Series is supported by the European Graduate School

ATROPOS PRESS
New York • Dresden

US: 151 First Avenue # 14, New York, N.Y. 10003
Germany: Mockritzer Str. 6, D-01219 Dresden

cover design: Hannes Charen

ISBN 978-0-9748534-8-2

CONTENTS

Chapter 1
Enter the Digital Dragon

Media technology has had a radical effect on the creative arts, and a very negative one in the eyes of many. Walter Benjamin argued that mechanical reproduction techniques, epitomised by photography, had drained the artwork of its power and aura[1]. Other social theorists from the Frankfurt School claimed that this had helped turn culture into an industry[2]. It is now taken for granted that today's still and video cameras, audio recorders and telecommunications devices have rendered traditional art forms essentially bankrupt and pointless as the primary means of directly representing the world[3], even if they are still esteemed for communicating less representational aspects of experience. The abstraction in art from the beginning of the 20th century onwards, and the emphasis on ephemeral and sensationalist art at the century's end[4], can be directly linked to this pressure from media technology. Now, at the beginning of the 21st century, electronic media gadgetry permeates our lives and representational art faces a continuing crisis.

But as the new Millennium matures, our creative urges are encountering their biggest challenge yet. The history of the Western world is often told as a story of technological achievement, from stone age to agricultural and then industrial revolutions. But only in the last couple of centuries has mankind consciously focused on its own technical ability as the primary goal of human life. The Eighteenth and Nineteenth Centuries ushered in the industrial age, where machines became man's finest accomplishment. The Twentieth Century was defined by

---

[1] *The work of art in the age of mechanical reproduction* in Walter Benjamin, *Illuminations* (New York: Schocken Books, 1969).
[2] *The Culture Industry: Enlightenment as Mass Deception* in Theodor Adorno and Max Horkheimer, *Dialectic of Enlightenment* (New York: Verso, 1997).
[3] Picasso was told his art was obsolete, because photography could show the world the way it really was. In response, he asked to see a picture of his interlocutor's wife and commented, "She's a bit small. And flat."
[4] For example, the Young British Artists popularized by the patronage of Charles Saatchi and his 1997 exhibition *Sensation*.

its exponentially increasing technological development – the automobile, jet air travel, the nuclear bomb, film and television, amongst many others. But in the last decades of the Twentieth Century, a new invention began to accelerate the rate of change, rapidly stretching out its influence into other areas of technology. It has influenced seemingly every corner of life, but in particular it has radically changed the media. This invention was of course the digital computer, a device which over 60 per cent of US households owned at the tail end of 2005[5].

Computer technology was originally devised in the first half of the Twentieth Century, primarily for signal processing in radio communications and wartime secret-code breaking[6]. But since that time it has become the quintessential general-purpose tool, applicable to almost any human activity. Digital algorithms have been used to improve the operation of every device, from cars to TVs to telephones. Nothing seems immune. No matter what task you wish to perform, computer enhancement will supposedly make it easier or better. Few other single technologies have had such a wide application, with such a revolutionary impact. Even era-changing developments like the steam engine or printing press have been confined to specific areas of life – such as travel, automated manufacture, or the democratisation of the written word. Digital computing, in contrast, promises to improve everything it touches – and it touches everything. Its implications are potentially as profound as the primal technology of writing itself.

As befits its signal processing origins, digital technology has had its greatest impact on communications systems and the media. The computer's skill at manipulating symbols has powered the Internet revolution, and radically changed the way all media are produced, even the 'old' print media. But how far can this

---

[5] US Census Bureau, October 2005
[6] Although Charles Babbage is usually credited with the first computer design in the 19th century, the currently dominant computing paradigm was very much a 20th century phenomenon. The work of Charles Babbage is only indirectly connected with the computing developments of Alan Turing and beyond, even though Turing was aware of Babbage's work.

process go? How much of our world view will we be willing or able to hand over to computerised mediation? And is there a limit to what these devices can do for us? Computers don't just enhance the power output of our cars, operate our washing machines more efficiently, or make it easier for us to type out correspondence. Digital technology has amplified the power of the media a hundredfold, and as a result has even had an impact on the arts. Traditional artistic tools – such as for drawing or for music making – can now be simulated digitally with ease. Instead of requiring the skill of a master, these tools are supposedly available to everyone. According to the software marketing literature, you don't need to be Picasso to paint with a PC, and anyone can find their inner Mozart via their Mac. More recently, the Internet has stepped in to provide a means of presenting artworks to audiences across the globe, potentially giving everyone a chance to be noticed. This is not just cynical marketing hype, either; there's a sincere belief amongst the creators of many of these tools that they are liberating people from the burden of having to learn the secrets of a craft. The ideology of computing is one of the democratisation of technique, in the same way that the printed word made reading available to the masses. The computer supposedly provides the technique itself, so all the user needs is raw ideas.

But this process of emancipation threatens to go further still. Computer software isn't just giving its users the tools to do something in the comfort of their studies, offices and 'dens' which they couldn't do before. Some programs supposedly can accomplish absolutely everything for you, including coming up with the ideas. All you need is to set a few initial parameters, then sit back while the computer itself performs the 'creative' work, such as composing your song or editing your home movie. This isn't a mere sales gimmick to make things more friendly for the non-technological user, in order to sell more products (although it often has that benefit) – it's an idea that has had an influence even in serious artistic circles. For example, in the mid 1990s musician Brian Eno used off-the-shelf software called Koan to develop a new kind of musical album. Eno's *Generative*

Music 1[7] was released on floppy disk. Instead of the disk containing recordings of the compositions, each track was a set of parameters for the Koan software, which would generate a slightly different variation on a basic musical theme each time the track was 'played'. To Eno, this seemed like the logical next step from the systems music he had been experimenting with since the beginning of his musical career.[8] Around the same time, visual artist William Latham was developing something similar in the field of graphics. Working at IBM, Latham had created an evolutionary system for 'growing' organic-looking images called Mutator, where the system itself came up with variations based on a set of seed parameters. The artist then chose one of these, from which a new set of mutations could be generated, and so on until a satisfactory artwork had been derived. Karl Sims of GenArts Inc has created gallery artworks evolved in a similar fashion as an interaction between computer and installation visitors[9].

These 1990s examples still foreground the human agency involved. In Eno's case, the artist is auteur of the seed parameters of the evolving music, and in Latham's case the artist is the godlike chooser of the 'fittest' mutation at each evolutionary stage of the growing artwork. But some artists have given their art-creating machines much greater autonomy. Harold Cohen's painting machine Aaron[10] draws its own pictures and is co-credited as the creator of the resulting works. Aaron and Cohen have even had joint art exhibitions, including at London's Tate Gallery. Ray Kurzweil, one of the leading evangelists of artificial intelligence, has created a system called

---

[7] Brian Eno, *Generative Music 1* (Sseyo, 1996)
[8] For example, Brian Eno and Robert Fripp, *No pussyfooting* (EG, 1973), or Eno's entire oeuvre of ambient works including *Music for airports* (EG, 1978).
[9] In 1997, Karl Sims developed the interactive installation *Galápagos* for the NTT InterCommunication Center in Tokyo. In this installation, viewers help evolve 3D animated creatures by selecting which ones will be allowed to live and produce new, mutated offspring.
[10] Aaron was developed at Stanford University's Artificial Intelligence Unit. Kurzweil CyberArt Technologies (www.kurzweilcyberart.com) has since created a screensaver product out of the Aaron technology.

Ray Kurzweil's Cybernetic Poet[11] which creates original new poetry based on the style of poems it has been fed as samples. David Link's Poetry Machine[12] similarly generates poetry by galvanising words and phrases from semantic links between a selection of classic texts, as if the machine itself were trying to express something.

But are any of these computer systems really creating art, or are they just executing a predefined program, albeit without previously predicted results? This would make the programmer the real artist, rather than the machine. If these computer systems are not really being creative, is this because the technology hasn't been developed sufficiently, or is there a more fundamental problem with the whole idea of computers making art? These kinds of questions have often been discussed in purely technical terms, taking for granted that a powerful-enough computer system could simulate any human faculty or quality, and then asking when a computer this powerful is likely to become available. For example, Ray Kurzweil argues that "Computers doubled in speed every three years at the beginning of the twentieth century, every two years in the 1950s and 1960s, and are now doubling in speed every twelve months. This trend will continue, with computers achieving the memory capacity and computing speed of the human brain by around the year 2020."[13] He then goes on to argue that conscious computers are entirely inevitable. Hans Moravec puts the date a little later at 2040, and even estimates the computing power of the human brain at 100,000,000 MIPS[14], or around 10,000 times the power of an average desktop computer in 2006. Traditional research into artificial intelligence has similarly focused on bringing together enough data and processing power to mimic the human mental faculty as a computational device, without paying much attention to whether or not the brain really does function

---

[11] Again, available from Kurzweil CyberArt Technologies.
[12] A description of the Poetry Machine can be found at http://www.medienkunstnetz.de/works/poetry-machine-1-0/.
[13] Ray Kurzweil, *The Age of Spiritual Machines* (London: Texere, 2001), p3.
[14] Hans Moravec, *Robot: Mere Machine to Transcendent Mind* (Oxford: Oxford University Press, 1999), p108.

exclusively in this way. More recently, attention has turned to less linear systems such as neural nets which can learn from their environment like people do, in the realisation that human knowledge is as much based on situational life experience as it is on having a coherent conceptualisation of the world and its rules.

But it's highly questionable whether artificial intelligence is just an issue of computational power. Although few at the forefront of computer science believe anymore that even a complex digital system models the exact working of the human brain, a similarly small number adequately question what computing represents in the history of technology. On the one hand, it is generally understood that if a computer could exhibit true human intelligence, then it would have profound impact on how we conceive ourselves as living beings. Our idea of what it means to be a human subject would be radically altered if we really knew how a human brain worked and could build one, instead of leaving it to the mysteries of sexual union. If a computer could devise original, creative artistic works of its own, the impact would be similar to discovering that the Earth was not the centre of the universe, or wasn't flat. Human beings would no longer be special in any way. As Ray Kurzweil argues[15], we would become inferior to our technological offspring. Given the exponential growth in computing power, our human bodies would soon be left behind as slower, obsolete models once we have downloaded ourselves into our cybernetic upgrades.

But this could be looking at the problem the wrong way round. Simply assuming the theoretical possibility of true artificial intelligence as a given, and then asking questions of what constitutes humanity because of this possibility, leaves some important concepts unexamined. There's no guarantee that computers which are faster than the human brain in terms of calculations per second will actually be conscious in the same way that we are. For a start, as John Searle has pointed out[16], much conventional research into artificial intelligence fails to

---

[15] Again, in Ray Kurzweil, *The Age of Spiritual Machines* (London: Texere, 2001).
[16] John R Searle, *The Mystery of Consciousness* (London: Granta Books, 1997).

tackle the concept of 'qualia', or inner subjective experience – and that is merely one example. So instead of discussion when and how computers will be powerful enough to transcend human intelligent, over the subsequent chapters I intend to reverse the focus, and explore what the assumption that artificial intelligence can and will be created by technological means says about the state of our culture. In the process I hope to show how the idea that machines could create art indicates a continuing metaphysical presupposition in Western society and an underlying misconception of what being human really entails. As the pinnacle of human technology, the computer is the ultimate product of metaphysics – the endpoint of "the triumphant progress of Western technology, which Heidegger cites as the third characteristic of the end of metaphysics, alongside the supremacy of the will and the view of the world as an image of man."[17] By questioning our intentions in developing computers and other artificial intelligence devices, I hope to show how they exemplify mankind's anthropomorphic projection of an image of itself onto the world. However, an enlightened approach to computerised intelligence which takes this on board could lead in a different direction, which will be outlined in the final chapter. If we reassess the intentions behind the crowning achievements of the technical programme – ie, devices which attempt to mimic our very consciousness – the process could radically change our view of subjectivity in the age of digital media. This reassessment would redefine the 'me' in the age of media. After all, if computers could somehow do truly creative work 'better' than humans, this would be the final triumph of alienation. It would represent the total disassociation of ourselves from ourselves by means of our own technological artefacts. So why exactly do we actually want to build machines which simulate and even surpass our own creative mental faculties in the first place?

---

[17] Wolfgang Schirmacher, *The End of Metaphysics – What does this mean?*, SOCIAL SCIENCE INFORMATION 23, 3 (1984), p603-609.

Chapter 2
The essence of art is not 'the arts'

Before discussing the deeper implications for humanity of computer-created art, we first need to get a handle on what exactly art is, and its more general relation to technology. In contemporary Western society, art and technology are often seen to be at odds. Both have their established niches in culture. These are kept quite separate, with a few notable exceptions such as MIT's Media Lab or the ZKM Center for Arts and Media in Karlsruhe, Germany. The development of new technology is concentrated around scientific research establishments, which are usually either state-funded academic institutions or corporate-owned labs, although the odd maverick inventor still manages to come up with influential new ideas on a smaller scale, such as the bagless vacuum cleaners invented by the UK's James Dyson. The results are the gadgets we buy to facilitate the various everyday activities of our lives. The arts, on the other hand, are usually developed at specialised art and design, drama or music schools, and can be found in the gallery or academy, at designated performance spaces, or they could be encountered in our living rooms. To the general public, the arts are primarily there for entertainment, decoration or depiction, intended to make life prettier or represent something we experience in our lives in a diverting way. Art isn't considered to be useful in the same way that technology is thought to be useful. If art has a use beyond being aesthetic, it's certainly not clear to most people what that use is. With the kinds of computing tools discussed in the introduction to this book, however, technology has been brought to bear on artistic endeavour in the same way that it has been called upon to achieve other 'more useful' tasks in life, like transportation or telecommunication. To do this, a conception of what art actually is will have been formulated by the creators of the technology, if not consciously then indirectly as a cultural assumption. Technology is always created with a specific end in mind, and if that end is making art, then art must have been defined at least loosely in advance.

So what exactly is art, and how does this differ from what it is conceived to be by technologists? Heidegger has argued in *The Question Concerning Technology* and *The Origin of the Work of Art* that art and technology in fact share a common origin. The Greek word τεχνη (*techne*) is the etymological source of all Western forms of technique, be they artistic skill, technological knowledge, or craftsmanship. Like the related word επιστεμη (*episteme*), *techne* refers to a certain kind of know-how, perhaps more ends-oriented than *episteme*, but still knowledge nonetheless. In particular, in *The Origin of the Work of Art*, Heidegger talks of the essence of art being a revealing-concealing truth and explains that the ancient Greek term αληθεια (*aletheia*) represents this process of truth:

> "It has often enough been pointed out that the Greeks, who knew a few things about works of art, use the same word, *techne*, for craft and art and call the craftsman and the artist by the same name: *technites* [] The word *techne* denotes rather a mode of knowing. To know means to have seen, in the widest sense of seeing, which means to apprehend what is present, as such. For Greek thought the essence of knowing consists in *aletheia*...the revealing of beings. *Techne*...is a bringing forth of beings in that it brings forth what is present as such out of concealment and specifically into the unconcealment of its appearance; *techne* never signifies the action of making. [] The artist is a *technites* not because he is also a craftsman, but because both the setting forth of works and the setting forth of equipment occur in a bringing forth that causes beings in the first place to come forward and be present in assuming an outward aspect."[18]

---

[18] *The Origin of the Work of Art* in Martin Heidegger, *Basic Writings* (London: Routledge, 1993), p184.

Unlike the conventional notion of truth as *adequatio*, or adequation, this isn't truth as defined by how similar a mental conception is to reality. The latter implies that a direct and unmediated connection to this reality is possible. Instead, truth as *aletheia* by its very nature highlights one area of reality whilst suppressing another. Truth as *adequatio* has been set up in opposition to art since Plato[19], and heightens the importance of the scientific knowledge lying behind technology. In contrast, truth as *aletheia* can be situated equally at the origin of both art and science. However, if art is a way of bringing out the truth of the world in the same way that technology as the setting forth of equipment is a way of bringing out the truth of the world, then it is conceivable that technology could work in perfect harmony with the arts. Technology could be used in a symbiotic way as part of the artistic process to amplify its effect, assisting in its programme of revealing.

This is, indeed, how computers are expected to be used – they supposedly help in the realisation of an artistic idea by liberating the user from the constraints of technique. But in this formulation, the artistic idea is in some way prior to the technological means of achieving it, and effectively appears independent. Conceiving of the part technology can play in the artistic process in this way falls directly into the trap recognised in Heidegger's famous theory that technology is in essence 'Enframing' – or framework, as the German word Ge-stell is sometimes translated[20]. Although technology is conventionally viewed as a neutral instrument or means to an end, Heidegger argues in *The Question Concerning Technology* that technology brings with it an embedded world view. So using technology

---

[19] However, *adequatio* has its artistic parallel in *mimesis*, which has been disparaged since Plato as a fake semblance of the real, rather than its faithful copy. This opposition of *adequatio* and *mimesis* is problematic, because of the lack of distinction between where one ends and the other begins. Why is a theory which conforms to perceived reality more acceptable than an artwork which mimics it, thereby bringing out the characteristics of reality? We will be discussing the repercussions of this mimetic view of the arts later in the chapter.

[20] For example, Joan Stambaugh substitutes Ge-Stell with 'The Framework' throughout her translation of Martin Heidegger, *Identity and Difference* (Chicago and London: The University of Chicago Press, 1969).

already encourages the user to see the world in a narrower way, one which is dictated by the technology itself. Similarly, using computer technology to make art already narrows the range of artistic choices available, and hence the kind of truth which can be revealed. For example, the user of a photograph retouching program will only be able to treat still images in certain predefined ways, even if the range of combinations possible is very large. Lev Manovich has described this new mode of creation in the digital age as database-driven[21]. However, it's questionable how different this is from any established technique brought to bear in making art, except in the degree of technology involved. Learning how to use oil paints is an acquired skill, in just the same way as learning to use the painting tools in a photo-editing program. Both skills impose a constraint on what the final product is likely to look like, with the artist choosing from a range of historically prior ways of doing things. Indeed, it could be argued that this is the concealing aspect of truth as *aletheia* at work. But, despite this constraint, in neither example is the output entirely predictable. As Jean-Luc Nancy argues in *The Muses*:

> "…'art' never appears except in a tension between two concepts of art, one technical and the other sublime – and this tension remains in general without concept."[22]

In other words, art is simultaneously a technique or craft which dictates a certain style, and something that cannot be so easily defined – a semi-blind fumbling for the sublime, with no clear prior conceptualisation of the end product. We will be discussing the implications of the sublime later in the essay. For our argument so far, we will merely consider how each new artwork is at the same time part of a genre, yet something special which transcends that genre:

---

[21] Lev Manovich, *The Language of New Media* (Cambridge, Massachussetts: The MIT Press, 2001).
[22] Jean-Luc Nancy, *The Muses* (Stanford: Stanford University Press, 1996), p4.

> "The *singular plural/singular* is the law and
> the problem of 'art', as it is of 'sense' or of the
> sense of the senses, of the sensed sense of the
> sensuous difference."[23]

As Nancy explains, no single art can entirely epitomise art in general, just as no single sense defines the paradigm of sensing. This can be reduced to a simple derivation from mathematics, which Nancy also shows. In set theory a single member does not make a set – there must always be more than one member to create the set. This tension between the example and the general group it's supposed to exemplify is a crucial element of the notion of identity we will be discussing in a later chapter. It's also a core part of recent neurological theory[24], where it is now believed that the inputs from the various senses are homogenised at a fairly low level of the brain, removing their distinction. Citing an example of a blind patient who can now 'see' with the highly concentrated touch senses of the tongue, Jeff Hawkins argues that the senses are essentially interchangeable at the more abstract levels of the neural system. So it would be ridiculous to argue that any one of the senses is in any way 'typical', although some take a more primary role under certain circumstances. Similarly, in line with Heidegger's conception of art as a way of bringing forth the world into Being, Nancy discusses the difference between art and artworks:

> "As soon as it takes place, 'art' vanishes; it is
> *an* art, the latter is *a* work, which is a style, a
> manner, a mode of resonance with other
> sensuous registers, a rhythmic reference back
> through indefinite networks."[25]

The activity of art creates artworks, which in their turn define genres. These become the context, the ground upon which the artistic process takes place. However, whilst studying the

---

[23] _, p13.
[24] As described in Jeff Hawkins, *On Intelligence* (New York: Times Books, 2004).
[25] Jean-Luc Nancy, *The Muses* (Stanford: Stanford University Press, 1996), p36.

artworks of the past aids the discovery of technique, this clearly misses an important part of the process. The truly creative activity of art escapes the finished artwork as soon as it is completed, and without it even the greatest technique is devoid of the originality which is also fundamental to art. It becomes a mere copy of what went before. As Heidegger argues:

> "Perhaps the 'ground' is only the *mimesis/methexis* according to which the arts or the senses of the arts endlessly meta-phorise each other."[26]

In studying artworks historically, the arts become like a dog chasing its tail, because analysing the end product of artistic activity never quite catches up with what exactly art is as it comes into being. This has profound implications for attempts to compute the artistic.

When seen in this context, programming a computer to make art by copying the technique behind existing artworks and genres seems to miss a crucial part of the process. It doesn't grasp the fully original nature of art. Artworks and genres – the various arts in general – are the by-products of art, and no single artwork nor group of artworks can epitomise the essence of the artistic in themselves. The art creation process may set up the arts, but it's not rigidly constrained within them once they have come into being. Not only genres within the arts, but every branch of the arts has had a finite history. For example, painting and paintings come from an act of painting, the technique of which has evolved considerably over an extremely long, but still finite, history. The origin of painting can be traced archaeologically to prehistoric caves. Pigments have been found in Zambia that are hundreds of thousands of years old. The oldest cave paintings date back over 35,000 years, although Nancy's example in *The Muses* of Lascaux in France is somewhere between 10,000 and 28,000 years old. Before the earliest cave paintings, it has been argued that bodies were the primary canvas for painting. But

---

[26] _, p24.

there would have been a time when there was no painting, just as there was a time when there was no mankind, according to the theory of evolution. As Heidegger argues, art is a bringing forth into being – and so at some point homo sapiens, or its ancestors, would have brought painting into being and, in locations such as Lascaux, through painting the technique of representing three-dimensional objects via a two-dimensional portrait. Certain traits of those objects – the horns of the bull in the Lascaux Hall of Bulls, for example – would have been brought out in the portrait. This highlighting of certain characteristics would have fundamentally altered the way the world was viewed by the artwork's creators and those who looked upon it.

> "'Art' is the beginning itself, and it traverses, like a single, immobile gesture, the twenty-five thousand years of the *animal monstrans*, of the *animal monstrum*. [] Art is but an immense tradition of the invention of the arts, of the birth of endless forms of knowledge."[27]

Similarly, Heidegger states: "In the work of art the truth of beings has set itself to work."[28] Just as technology enframes our world view, art can influence it in another direction, developing new frames. This is perfectly in line with our argument that both have a common origin in the *techne* of Greek antiquity.

Art happens

Hegel thought art was no longer the highest form of truth[29], and Nancy argues in *The Muses* that Hegel's notion of art still remains the most definitive one today: "...there is a definition of art that encompasses all the others (for the West at least, but art

---

[27] _, p71.
[28] *The Origin of the Work of Art* in Martin Heidegger, *Basic Writings* (London: Routledge, 1993), p162.
[29] "Art no longer counts for us as the highest manner in which truth obtains existence for itself." Georg Wilhelm Friedrich Hegel, *Lectures on aesthetics* (London: Penguin, 1993). For Hegel, art had become another expression of the concrete universal, of substance becoming subject.

is a Western concept). It is, not at all by chance, Hegel's definition: art is the *sensible presentation of the Idea.*[30] Such a definition is still perfectly compatible with the notion that art is primarily aesthetic in intent, designed to give pleasure through its formal appearance to the senses in its presentation. However, Nancy argues that today art has become a vestige or trace, and is no longer the presentation of an internal world of ideals, but an expression of the non-ideal. Nancy's thesis that the truth in art is a vestige has been incarnated within contemporary art in the move towards abstraction, which we touched upon in Chapter 1.

> "That art is today its own vestige, this is what
> opens us to it. It is not a degraded presentation
> of the Idea, nor the presentation of a degraded
> Idea; it presents what is not 'Idea': motion,
> coming, passage, the going-on of coming-to-
> presence."[31]

In other words, art continues to pursue the embodiment of the artistic, in the greater realisation that the resulting artwork is simply a trace pointing indeterminately beyond itself, and can never fully achieve its goal. In fact, this has become the very focus of attention in many cases, as we will discuss shortly. Just as Schopenhauer famously described music as "pure will" due to its non-representational abstraction[32], so contemporary art chases after its own self as presentation – the "reception of its own receptivity"[33], in Nancy's words. This is art about the process of art itself. Yves-Alain Bois has discussed in *Painting as Model* how the works of Piet Mondrian and Barnett Newman attempt to

---

[30] Jean Luc-Nancy, *The Muses* (Stanford: Stanford University Press, 1996), p88
[31] _, p98
[32] Nietzsche states in *The birth of tragedy* (New York: Doubleday, 1956), p97:
"Schopenhauer assigned to music a totally different character and origin from all the other arts, because it does not, like all the others, represent appearance, but the will directly." He also cites Schiller: "With me the perception has at first no clear or definite object; this is formed later. A certain musical mood comes first, and the poetical idea only follows later."
[33] Jean Luc-Nancy, *The Muses* (Stanford: Stanford University Press, 1996), p29

subvert form and the distinction between figure and ground[34]. He argues that even Matisse's paper cut-outs do this to some extent by dispensing with the traditional process of pencil-drawing an outline and then colouring it in, which inscribes the form/content dichotomy into the method of artistic production itself – and also makes form (drawing the outline) more important than content (colouring it in). A significant proportion of art during the last 100 years has reassessed the balance between figure and ground, thereby questioning what is figure and what is ground – particularly the work of Barnett Newman and his 'zips', some of which are wider than what is ostensibly their background. However, questioning figure and ground wasn't Newman's primary goal, more a side effect. As Lyotard argues about Newman: "The message is the presentation, but it presents nothing; it is, that is, presence. This 'pragmatic' organisation is much closer to an ethics than to any aesthetics or poetics."[35] In other words, it points beyond its concrete material expression towards moral tenets which cannot be grasped by direct literal description.

We'll be taking the latter implication further in the last chapter. For our argument so far, it is this message of presence, the "it happens", which must be singled out. Jackson Pollock's "all-over" painting asks similar questions about coming-to-presence as Newman's zips. But by throwing into a number of his works what is ostensibly rubbish, such as cigarette butts[36], Pollock takes the argument another step further. Not only is the formal interplay of figure and ground blurred, but what constitutes form itself is taken to task. However, Marcel Duchamp has been the true master of this particular line of artistic argument. His "readymade" works fundamentally question what can be

---

[34] Discussing Mondrian's *New York City*, Bois states that the painter instantly avoids "any form being able to take root there or getting caught up in the woof of the painting." Newman's *Onement I*, on the other hand, "allowed him to dismiss altogether...the structure figure/ground, which constitutes, as much as our being situated, the basis of our perception." Yve-Alain Bois, *Painting as Model* (Cambridge, Massachussetts: The MIT Press, 1990).

[35] *Newman: The Instant* in Jean-Francois Lyotard, *The Inhuman* (Stanford: Stanford University Press, 1991), p81.

[36] For example, Jackson Pollock, *Blue Poles: Number 11, 1952.*

considered an artistic form, although they don't dispense with material reference in the way that Newman's oeuvre does. In fact, it is crucial in works like Duchamp's *Fountain* that the subject be clearly recognised as an everyday urinal. In this way, art is wrenched back into life from its previously quasi-religious ivory tower. At the most extreme end of the scale, one could also add the many cases of excrement being used in 20th Century art – from Gilbert and George's *Shitted* and *The Naked Shit Pictures* to Andres Serrano's *Piss Christ* and Chris Ofili's elephant dung-laden portraits. In the case of these works, shit really does happen.

The theme of formlessness in contemporary art, as typified by much of Pollock's opus, shows the differentiation between figure and ground all but eradicated. The formless[37] shows how even when not only representational meaning, but any recognisable form at all, is removed it's still possible to discern something at work – there is still a presentation. The formless in art continues to have a discernible wilfulness about it – it's not just random, even if the process by which it is created often has elements which emulate randomness. "Emulate" is a key term here, with its resonance for the concepts of mimesis and simulacra. As we will be discussing in later sections on computing and subjectivity, the randomness in the process merely supplies possibilities – the artist still chooses amongst those possibilities, and still brings human judgement to bear. However, it would be wrong to equate the "it happens" of the formless purely with the human hand at work in it. Indeed, "it happens" in the artwork as much to the artist as it does to the viewer. The fact that the agency in the artwork is human is not as significant as the fact that there is agency at all, and whether or not the human aspect of this agency is entirely necessary remains in question.

So what is it that differentiates the formless artwork from something purely random? Stripped of specific material subjects, the subject matter of the formless points towards the question of

---

[37] Yve-Alain Bois and Rosalind E Kraus, *Formless* (New York: Zone Books, 2000) offers a comprehensive guide to this theme in modern art.

Being itself – the constant examination of how there is something and not nothing. Art as vestige or trace is art rarefied to its essence, where gesture and pure presentation become divorced from material representation.[38] In Hegel's terms, art has become the presentation of the pure Idea, which is no longer the Idea *of* something in the world – art is now the presentation of the Idea of Idea-ness itself, a pure expression of the faculty of consciousness. Against the grounding backdrop of its own history, the activity of making art becomes its own figure. For, indeed, ground is nothing but congealed figure – the historical memory of past figures.[39] Formless art communicates through the human sense that *there is something there* beyond the material world, but leaves exactly what that something is undefined. Kant argued that the aesthetic sense of taste similarly functions in a way which is prior to conception:

> "One could even define taste as the faculty of judging what renders our feeling, proceeding from a given representation, universally *communicable* without the mediation of a concept."[40]

So how could one go about defining the technique of the formless artwork, or building a technology to create it? This would seem problematic using tools which are the direct product of clear, fully formed conceptualisation. As Lyotard argues with regards to communications technology: "what about communication without concept at a time when, precisely, the 'products' of technologies applied to art cannot occur without the massive and hegemonic intervention of the concept?"[41] In fact, modern abstract art is popularly criticised for its seeming

---

[38] "The transimmanence, or patency, of the world takes place as art, as works of art." Jean-Luc Nancy, *The Muses* (Stanford: Stanford University Press, 1996), p35.

[39] Heidegger argues along similar lines in *On The Essence of Ground* in Martin Heidegger, *Pathmarks* (Cambridge: Cambridge University Press, 1998).

[40] Emmanuel Kant, *Critique of Judgement* (New York: Dover Publications, 2005), §40.

[41] Jean-Francois Lyotard, *The Inhuman* (Stanford: Stanford University Press, 1991), p109.

lack of technique – the "anyone could do that" syndrome – as well as its lack of direct representation of physical objects. Many contemporary works provoke almost violent dislike in some (usually politically conservative) sections of the general public, who consider this kind of artwork not only formless, but also therefore pointless. This popular criticism is not as puerile as it first appears, as indeed the paradox evinced by modern art is distinctly between what *could* happen and what *does* – the struggle between the conceptual world of ideas and their realisation, or perhaps even between Being and beings, as Heidegger might have put it. The argument that "anyone could do that" is a symptom of Western metaphysics, and is linked to an inability to reconcile finite being with infinite Being, subjects we will be returning to in later chapters. The emphasis on pure technique in the arts and the disavowal of raw originality is a more refined version of this irreconcilability. Emphasis on technique is anthropocentric. It puts its faith entirely in human agency. But the converse – discounting the importance of the viewer – is still a mistake. The viewing subject is still that which art acts *through*.

However, as we argued earlier with reference to Nancy's *The Muses*, technique is only half of art. So what exactly is the other, sublime portion Nancy talks about? Kant, in his *Critique of Judgement*, considered the workings of the sublime in art, and tellingly prophesied what was to come in the 20th Century art world. Kant's idea of "negative presentation" as a means of representing the absolute, Lyotard argues, "prefigures the Minimalist and abstractionist solutions painting will use to try and escape the figurative prison".[42] By introducing a sense of *being beyond limits* into aesthetics, the sublime takes artistry beyond the merely mimetic exposition of form, and hence beyond the representational. In Kant's conception, the sublime *evokes* the ineffable rather than representing it concretely, which he considers logically impossible. Modern art attempts something similar, even if the ineffable that is being evoked is no longer God but perhaps a more secular Being. It's hard to

---

[42] *Newman: The Instant* in Jean-Francois Lyotard, *The Inhuman* (Stanford: Stanford University Press, 1991), p85.

imagine that computers, programmed to mimic human techniques, could have any ability at all in evoking something ineffable, as they are primarily concerned with the effable – calculating concrete values from input data which has been clearly defined in advance.

Herein lies the double bind of using computers to make art in the contemporary, post-representational art world. Computers operate on what happens, which presupposes that something which can be clearly defined is happening in the first place. But the mystery exposed in art is that something happens at all, and in art one finds an exploration of and participation within *happening* itself. As Lyotard argues:

> "Before asking questions about what it is and about its significance, before the *quid*, it must 'first' so to speak 'happen', *quod*. That it happens 'precedes', so to speak, the question pertaining to what happens."[43]

As we will be discussing in the next chapter, the metaphysical origins of technology epitomised in computers turn presence into a thing – event (quod) into "eventity" (quid). This is an absolute necessity for the kind of calculating operations which a binary computational device performs. The stuff of raw experience needs to be concretely pre-conceptualised (by a human being who is programming the computer) before it can be operated upon. This situates computing in a place that is always "after the fact". Information technology and indeed all media technology works with *re*-presentation, and hence is always at least one step removed from the *presentation* involved in art and aesthesis. In Lyotard's words:

> "The question raised by the new technologies in connection with their relation to art is that of the 'here and now'. What does 'here' mean on the phone, on television, at the receiver of

---

[43] Jean-Francois Lyotard, *The Inhuman* (Stanford: Stanford University Press, 1991), p90.

an electronic telescope? And the 'now'? Does not the 'tele-' element necessarily destroy presence, the 'here-and-now' of the forms and their 'carnal' reception? What is a place, a moment, not anchored in the immediate 'passion' of what happens? Is a computer in any way here and now? Can anything *happen* with it? Can anything happen *to* it?"[44]

Putting aside the rhetorical flourish of Lyotard's questions, there is clearly still a here and now in the usage of computers. But it is a presence that is much more heavily mediated and premeditated than less technological forms of interaction with the world. The fundamental question is whether this is a new form of existence, or just a rarefied version of elements which have always existed in human life. After all, humans have always seen the world through mediating senses, rather than "directly", if such a thing can be conceptualised without thinking of sight, sound and smell sitting in between. However, whilst the five senses were developed by the "blind watchmaker"[45] of evolution, the new tele-senses of digital media are the very deliberate product of human ingenuity.

Art emitters, art receivers

Describing art creation as an evocation of the pure Idea makes of it a practice which drags the Idea kicking and screaming into the material, social world. This naturally forces us to consider the viewer of the artwork. Taken from the artist's perspective alone, the Idea of the artwork remains a concept in the mind of the artist, and could be purely subjective. Only in its engagement with a viewer does the artwork's ability to truly evoke something concrete from its conceptualisation come into play. But it can't be taken for granted that the artist's conceptualisation is the

---

[44] _, p118.
[45] In *The Blind Watchmaker* (London: Penguin Books, 2006), Richard Dawkins argues that evolution has no design, and needs none, to create wonders such as the eye.

same as the viewer's more concrete evocation. All that can be said is that something in the work engages the viewer – it doesn't necessarily have to be what was intended. Roland Barthes' late work *Camera Lucida* discusses the various levels in which we engage with photographs, considered to be the archetypal mechanical artwork by Walter Benjamin[46] and Vilem Flusser[47]. For Barthes, the intended subject of the photograph is called the Spectrum. Within this, the Adventure is one photograph's ability to grab attention when another doesn't. The Studium refers to the cultural view of a photo – its "average affect" for most who experience it. However, Barthes talks about a third level on which a photo works, which he calls the Punctum. This is the photo's ability to affect in a way which transcends the programmed cultural response. In Barthes' own words, "A photograph's punctum is that accident which pricks me"[48] Later in *Camera Lucida*, he elaborates further:

> "...a detail attracts me. I feel that its mere presence changes my reading, that I am looking at a new photograph, marked in my eyes with a higher value. This 'detail' is the punctum. It is not possible to posit a rule of connection between the studium and the punctum (when it happens to be there). It is a matter of co-presence, that is all one can say..."[49]

Barthes argues that the Punctum, the element of a photograph which touches you personally and singularly, is an important part of how a photograph gains its emotional impact for a specific viewer. This singular affect is potentially an element of the creative artistic process itself, albeit perhaps an unintended one. An *event* like this in the photograph, which forms part of its

---

[46] *The Work of Art in the Age of Mechanical Reproduction* in Walter Benjamin, *Illuminations* (New York: Schocken Books, 1969).

[47] Vilem Flusser, *Towards a Philosophy of Photography* (London: Reaktion Books, 2000).

[48] Roland Barthes, *Camera Lucida* (London: Vintage, 1993), p27

[49] _, p42

presentation, is what the photographic artist also uses to discern appropriate qualities in a work he or she is creating. In *Camera Lucida*, Barthes is discussing photographs purely from the point of view of spectator, but artists clearly take the posture of a spectator of their own works during the process of creation, and afterwards. This *speculative distance* in the act of creation is an important point we'll consider at the end of this chapter, and also when we discuss in detail the use of generative artificial intelligence systems in creating art. Returning to Nancy:

> "But what does art do if not finally touch upon and touch by means of the principal heterogeneity of 'sensing'? In this heterogeneity in principle that resolves itself into heterogeneity *of the* principle, art touches on the sense of touch itself: in other words, it touches at once on the 'self-touching' inherent in touch and on the 'interruption' that is no less inherent in it."[50]

The coming-to-consciousness inherent in perceiving art, or indeed all sensing, is as much a consciousness of self as it is of the world. There is always a concomitant realisation of separation between the two. Perhaps Barthes best sums up the difference between culturally ascribed meaning and the personal meaning brought out by the Punctum when he says: "The studium is ultimately always coded, the punctum is not... What I can name cannot really prick me."[51] The Punctum is therefore like a trauma, which gains its dramatic effect by exceeding the linguistic code, similar in nature to Virilio's notion of the *general accident.*[52] However, Heidegger talks of an event of appropriation, Ereignis, which is a process whereby the accidentally encountered is brought back into the circle of Being. This could be considered the juncture between Studium and Punctum. Ereignis is something artists and art viewers have in

---

[50] Jean-Luc Nancy, *The Muses* (Stanford: Stanford University Press, 1996), p18.
[51] Roland Barthes, *Camera Lucida* (London: Vintage, 1993), p51.
[52] *The State of Emergency* in Paul Virilio, *The Virilio Reader*, ed James Der Derian (Oxford: Blackwell, 1998).

common. Heidegger argues that the viewer participates in the artwork via an event of appropriation, and this is how an artwork maintains its power through historical epochs. Hence, he coins the term 'art preservers'[53], because an artwork's status as artwork is maintained by its continuing ability to provoke Ereignis – or, in Barthes's terms, by the recurrence of a Punctum within it for successive generations, even if the substance of this Punctum varies through time. The artist and the art preserver have the artwork itself in common, a material thing which is open to concrete conceptualisation once it has been created. But this thing evokes a community of experience in itself, and this is what gives it power as a historical entity. As Kant argued, the community of experience and its evocation are prior to conceptualisation – they cannot be pinned down as concrete concepts, only hinted at. Heidegger states that each viewer participates in Ereignis and recreates it anew:

> "Just as a work cannot be without being created, but is essentially in need of creators, so what is created cannot itself come into being without those who preserve it."[54]

Returning to our core topic of computerised artistic creativity, the locus of the problem has moved from the act of making a work to the ability to see something of importance in what has been made. This calls to mind the old adage about monkeys tapping away on typewriters and eventually coming up with the works of Shakespeare, purely by accident. Theoretically, this is entirely possible with enough monkeys and enough time, but (as

[53] However, being an art preserver is not an entirely personal affair: "Preserving the work does not reduce people to their private experiences, but brings them into affiliation with the truth happening in the work. Thus it grounds being for and with one another as the historical standing-out of human existence in relation to unconcealment." *The Origin of the Work of Art* in Martin Heidegger, *Basic Writings* (London: Routledge, 1993), p193. Barthes' punctum should perhaps always be considered to be fleeting and immediately on its way to studium – the personal affect in the work which through truth (as *aletheia*) transforms the cultural view of the photograph.
[54] *The origin of the work of art* in Martin Heidegger, *Basic Writings* (London: Routledge, 1993), p191.

with the "anyone could do that" critical argument discussed above) it's missing the important point that human life is finite. We'd never have enough monkeys or time. But even that is not taking into account the monkeys' inability to actually recognise if they had created great English drama. The chances are they would eat their works of genius before they were discovered, or at least throw the bits of paper about the cage. Similarly, computers could come up with great artworks purely at random, but how would they be able to tell the difference between these and output that would strike no chord whatsoever in a human viewer? This is clearly a matter of taste, and the problem therefore becomes how to program taste digitally. So we arrive at the question of what taste actually is, and closely allied concepts such as style and tact.

A matter of taste

As Philippe Lacoue-Labarthe discusses in *The Echo of the Subject*[55], a certain musicality prefigures subjectivity. A rhythmic pattern beats out the style of the subject, and Lacuoe-Labarthe argues that tact could be seen as this personal beat finding harmony in the immediate social fabric. Artistic taste is closely related to this conception of tact. Much work has been performed on areas of pattern recognition during research into machine intelligence (again a subject we will be returning to in a later chapter). However, tact and taste are done an injustice if viewed simply as pattern recognition. The implication is that the 'right' pattern has always existed and simply must be seen. This is clearly another example of truth as adequation, and as we have already discussed this notion of truth is particularly insufficient for a definition of artistic creativity. However, art shouldn't be seen as pattern production either. Instead, if we conceptualise truth as *aletheia*, art becomes more a process of pattern revealing – the pattern was there before it was brought out, but it certainly isn't the only pattern which could be found under different circumstances. Again, the spectre of arbitrary choice, of brute

---

[55] This essay can be found in Philippe Lacoue-Labarthe, *Typography* (Stanford: Stanford Univserity Press, 1989).

decision, can be felt. "The absolute is never there, never given in a presentation, but it is always 'present' as a call to think beyond the 'there'. Ungraspable, but unforgettable. Never restored, never abandoned."[56] Art is not the absolutely right pattern, nor is it the pattern which fits best, but it is a strongly resonant pattern which was brought out at that particular time by that particular artist, for reasons which are very particular to that artist. This singularity is what is so hard to replicate in a machine. "In the analytic of taste, sensation no longer has any cognitive finality; it no longer gives any information about an object but only about the 'subject' itself."[57] A computer must always have a prior reason for its choices, whereas the artistic reason is to be found in the process of choice itself. This goes beyond the artist to all those involved in the selection of art for public display. As Slavoj Zizek says of the art exhibition:

> "When we visit an exhibition today, we are thus not directly observing works of art – what we are observing is the curator's notion of what art is; in short, the ultimate artist is not the producer but the curator, his activity of selection."[58]

Linking this back to the generative artworks discussed in the first chapter, the artist him or herself has taken up a role more like a curator than a traditional artist. The computer is called upon to come up with ideas via a quasi-random process, after which the artist simply chooses the ones he or she likes. The real question, then, is what drives the action of choice. Clearly, choice is highly situational and depends on the interaction between the creator, the object, and (when the work is exhibited) the exhibition curator and viewers. Gregory Ulmer's work on

---

[56] Jean-Francois Lyotard, *Lessons on the Analytic of the Sublime* (Stanford: Stanford University Press, 1994), p150.
[57] Jean-Francois Lyotard, *Lessons on the Analytic of the Sublime* (Stanford: Stanford University Press, 1994), p9.
[58] Slavoj Zizek, *The Ticklish Subject* (London: Verso, 1999), p337.

writing strategies and heuretics[59] (the logic of creativity) emphasises the creative power of the homonym and other word games in literary authorship. Taking his cue from Derrida, Ulmer argues that the process at play in writing follows a route where superficial links – for example, differently spelled words which sound the same – can force meanings together, or build new ones. Like Barthes' Punctum, this process can also evoke resonance and nuances in the receiver which were not originally intended. Or, at least, the meaning of a work can be rendered unstable and prone to change through unpredictable, unintentional associations taking place in the mind of the 'art preserver'.

In this way, the possibilities generated by a computerised art creation system can have emotional effects and meanings for the artist and the viewer of the final work which are outside what was intended in the design of the system itself. Marcel Duchamp's concept of the Readymade has been playing off a similar idea for decades. Whether seen from the point of view of creator or viewer, however, the experience of an artwork always seems to contain an element of speculative thought. There's always a stepping back to consider what has been created, which brings it into the realm of the theoretical. The theoretical imperative in art is linked to the traditional belief that art imitates nature mimetically rather than coming directly from it.

The spectre of the imitative

So far, we have considered the essence of the artistic, and found it to be more of an evocative absence than anything conducive to systematic definition. But this is not the model of the arts habitually found in computerised art creation systems. Instead, such computer systems tend to copy traditional, non-computerised artistic techniques and forms – implying a very old-fashioned conception of what art is. As we discussed earlier,

---

[59] These concepts are discussed in Gregory Ulmer, *Heuretics* (Baltimore and London: The Johns Hopkins University Press, 1994) and *Applied Grammatology* (Baltimore and London: The Johns Hopkins University Press, 1985).

the view of art as mimetic in nature is deeply ingrained in Western culture (see footnote 19 above). In this conception, art copies the form of nature, creating a simulation of it. The view owes its philosophical origin to Plato and Aristotle. As the latter states, "on one hand techne accomplishes what phusis [nature] is incapable of effecting; on the other hand, techne imitates phusis."[60] Plato cast actors – and with them, artists in general – out of his ideal state for their dissimulation of nature. He argued that their mimicry of the natural was little more than lying. For Plato, artistic mimesis must have represented a double removal from the truth. Plato's famous allegory of the cave in *The Republic* describes how those without knowledge of his Forms were only seeing the shadows cast by the underlying structure of nature. Artists, epitomised by the tragic actor, would therefore be mimicking the shadows cast as outer appearance by the Forms, copying the copy so to speak.[61]

Plato is arguing that art is by nature mimesis – a form of mirroring – and Heidegger echoes this in his passages on the subject in *Nietzsche*. However, Heidegger goes further than Plato and calls artists themselves "mirrorers" (Spiegelers). Such mirror-bearing gives the artist an active role in the process of aletheia, the revealing and concealing in the artwork. But, like Plato's mimesis, Heidegger's use of the mirror metaphor externalises the process at work in art, and implies that it is a transparent, neutral reflection. The conception that art is a mirror paves the way for art to be mechanised, by reducing it to another form of passive, speculative observation separated from subjectivity. If art is an external process of reflection, its processes could in theory be captured and calculated, as Michel Foucault has argued is the way all human social institutions have developed historically. Indeed, that is essentially what the art academies attempt to do. Because of its conduciveness to such

---

[60] Aristotle, *Physics Books I-IV* (Harvard: Loeb Classical Library, 1986).
[61] As Gregory Ulmer argues, "When it becomes apparent in the work of the sophists that artistic presentations could persuade in the absence of truth, philosophy broke with literature, the consequences of which are still with us today and whose history may be traced in the fortunes of the two styles – the plain (scientific) and the rhetorical (literary)." *Applied Grammatology* (Baltimore and London: The Johns Hopkins University Press, 1985), p160.

formal analysis, art as mimetic speculation is what has been incorporated by computer science. The tools have been designed to ape the processes of conventional, representational art. This isn't necessarily a result of a weak understanding of aesthetics, so much as being dictated by the capabilities of the computer, as we will discuss in the next chapter. Still, the computer's power as a means of mirroring is without question. Modern technology, when applied to the task of mimesis, has resulted in copies that are becoming ever more indistinguishable from the real. The technology of 3D animation, in particular, has spawned "virtual reality", which nevertheless remains uncannily *not* reality despite its increasingly close resemblance to it.[62] There's something intrinsically circular about this whole process. Even though our imagination is often called upon in the cinema to conjure alien worlds or other impossible experiences, this is generally achieved through increasingly believable simulations of reality. Closer copies of human hair and skin are combined with intricate physical calculations of how explosions really work to make us suspend our disbelief just that little bit more during even more far-fetched situations. There's a clear longing to recreate nature itself, except this time perfectly under our control.

This full circle ironically echoes the social programme that was set in motion by Rousseau, who yearned for a return to an idealised golden age of natural mankind. His programme was rarefied by Schiller and Holderlin into the desire to return to "being Greek". As Lacoue-Labarthe argues in *Holderlin and the Greeks*[63], the essentially Greek state of nature probably never existed – it's a fiction or myth constructed by philosophers and social theorists to serve their ideologies about what constitutes mankind's destiny. Even Heidegger's existentialist return to the first philosophical principles of the pre-Socratics could be seen

---

[62] But as Lev Manovich argues, the majority of 3D animation is not "virtual reality". Instead, it remains within the borders of a frame created by the viewing screen, so is merely an extension of the 2D perspective image developed in painting and mechanized with the photograph. Lev Manovich, *The Language of New Media* (Cambridge, Massachussetts: The MIT Press, 2001).

[63] This essay can be found in Philippe Lacoue-Labarthe, *Typography* (Stanford: Stanford Univserity Press, 1989).

in this light, particularly his arcane references to a "distant dispensation"[64]. Similarly, the mimetic view of art has had a fundamental effect on Western culture, and is inextricably linked to our ontological metaphysics. There is a distinct paradox in this deep-rooted attempt to enlist consciousness in its own destruction, utilising thinking so that we might return to a romanticised time when we acted without thinking, in total accordance with our nature and our bodies.

But can consciousness ever return us to a state of oneness with "it happens"? Perhaps it is man's nature in fact to be artificial, to bring speculative imagination to bear on the natural and consciously coax from it something of the Idea. This is what Wolfgang Schirmacher is indicating with his co-option of the phrase "artificial life", and his argument that man is no longer merely the thinker, maker, or creator within the world. Instead, Schirmacher argues that through technologies such as virtual reality and genetics man has become the "generator" of his or her own world. With the growing potential to program our own bodily code, this worldly control goes right down to the level of the corporeal. Yet, even in this radical empowerment of man by technology, there is the need to return to the raw "it happens" of the body:

> "Homo generator's body politics is to SEE/
> HEAR/ SMELL/ TOUCH/ TASTE/ THINK
> before you act, it claims aesthetic perception
> as the basis of comprehending and
> interaction."[65]

The true paradox here is that just when it appears metaphysics has won out over physics – because man's Idea has become so powerful that it can generate reality – we are being urged to return to our carnal experience. Art is important here, because it is the quintessential example of humans working directly on

---

[64] Heidegger's "distant dispensation" is analysed by Hugo Ott in *Martin Heidegger: A Political Life* (London: Fontana, 1994).
[65] Wolfgang Schirmacher, *HOMO GENERATOR: Militant Media & Postmodern Technology*, http://www.egs.edu/faculty/schirmacher/homo.html (1994).

their own senses – the pure process of aesthesis. While natural phenomena can be sublimely aesthetic (the awesome beauty of a Swiss mountain range, for example) it is the artwork expressing that aesthesis which bears mankind's contribution. In the process, aesthetics is turned into a thing, as Heidegger argues in *The origin of the work of art*. This defining of an artwork as a thing is problematic. Just for starters, the nature of things has been conceptualised in more than one form. Heidegger argues that there are three basic conceptions of the thing: the thing as bearer of its characteristics, the thing as "aestheton" perceptible by our senses, and the thing as matter with a form (*hyle* and *morphe* in the original Greek) resulting in an outward appearance (*eidos*). The latter is the most relevant for our analysis of art.[66] As we discussed at the beginning of this chapter, however, Heidegger considers none of these definitions sufficient for the process he sees in the artwork of *bringing form into being*, but also bringing matter into Being. "The artwork opens up in its own way the Being of beings." This is how he concludes that "Art is truth setting itself to work."[67]

So art changes our world view. It's not just the attribution of form to matter, so much as bringing out the form *already within* matter. Sculptors in particular talk of how a specific piece of material – say a hunk of granite intended for sculpture – inspires the very form that is created out of it by their labour.[68] Contrary to the oft-encountered dichotomy between theory and practice, artistic activity always contains within it a speculative element. Both the artist and the viewer participate in this speculative experience emanating from the artwork, at different stages in its lifecycle. But in Heidegger's formulation the aesthetic moment precedes speculation about what it is:

---

[66] "The distinction of matter and form is the conceptual schema which is used, in the greatest variety of ways, quite generally for all art theory and aesthetics.[] Where does the matter-form structure have its origin - in the thingly character of the thing or in the workly character of the artwork?", *The origin of the work of art* in Martin Heidegger, *Basic Writings* (London: Routledge, 1993), p153.

[67] _, p165.

[68] British sculptress Barbara Hepworth said this of her materials, and even Michelangelo's unfinished sculptures are said to look as if they are themselves trying to escape out of the very rock from which they were hewn.

"To submit to this displacement means to transform our accustomed ties to world and earth and henceforth to restrain all usual doing and prizing, knowing and looking, in order to stay within the truth that is happening in the work."[69]

As we argued earlier, what is speculated isn't necessarily the same for the artist as it is for the viewer. With speculation, the artwork already becomes distant, an object of conceptualised thought. However, it is the product of speculation which is simulated in computerised art creation – the theory of what the artwork is trying to achieve. Computers recreate art theory very well, because they can learn its rules retrospectively. But this (aping Plato's cave) is chasing the shadows rather than replicating the shadow casters.

Art is the ultimate form of Althusser's "theoretical praxis", where theory and practice supposedly join forces. But even here our conception of the artistic finds itself enslaved to a preconception. The speculative distance of theory in artwork is derived from the priority given to the senses of sight and hearing in *theoria*, with its general derivation from *theoros*, meaning spectator. This speculative distance is in fact alien to the activity of art creation. For a start the art process involves, if not all the senses, then more than just sight and hearing – the feeling of touching the musical instrument, the tangibility and smell of painting or sculpture. The artist is involved in something greater than what ends up being conceptualised in the work as a primarily visual or auditory entity. However, the *theoria* of art is what is simulated in computing. It is often found that trying to use a computer to make art forces the artist into a contemplative mode, devoid of visceral interaction or full involvement in the art-creating process. The system is geared towards having a theoretical artistic idea first, then using the computer as a tool to realise it. This two-stage approach is clearly in opposition to the

---

[69] *The origin of the work of art* in Martin Heidegger, *Basic Writings* (London: Routledge, 1993), p191.

way the artistic process actually breaks the boundaries of the senses and of genres, as Nancy argues in *The Muses*. Computerised art, despite its hybrid "multimedia" image, is by its very nature forced into a genre, because it is intrinsically based upon the simulation of genres. The process of art as truth is reversed. Instead of the concept of the artwork coming through the work itself, the work comes from the concept.

The dominance of *theoria* and contemplation in computer art, and *theoria*'s reliance on sight and hearing, shows how computers are a product of logocentrism. Derrida's grammatology, as described by Ulmer in *Applied Grammatology*, attempts to bring the non-verbal to bear on writing, but the latter remains a speculative, visual thing. It is "observed from a vantage point", considering the root "speculat-", which in turn derives from *specula* (Latin for watchtower). Even Schopenhauer and Nietzsche contribute to the primacy of hearing with their championing of music as the wilful antidote to the metaphysical word. Hearing is still given primacy and the (visual) written word relegated to its secondary record, with taste, smell and touch discarded entirely. This is also seen in the arts, with only a few modern works engaging the latter three senses, despite the fact that throughout history art has been created in a process which involves much more than just sound and vision. Even playing a musical instrument has a visceral quality. The concept of art, as in fine art, is generally used to refer to the visual arts, with their passive lack of involvement which both Kant and Hegel preferred. The visual arts aren't used up by the viewer, who simply stands back and looks.

So computers map the theoretical, speculative aspect of art, without addressing the full gamut of corporeal involvement found in creativity. The traditional view of art as mimesis already pushes it into a position once removed from direct connection with reality, turning it into a speculative enterprise. But as our analysis of abstraction and the formless above has shown, art is never just a weak reflection of the real. Nietzsche states: "Art is not an imitation of nature, but its metaphysical supplement, raised up beside it in order to overcome it."[70] Art is a form of aletheia – it foregrounds aspects (eidos) of the real and highlights them over others, and is thus fundamentally a process of truth. But the aspects brought into the foreground are still a function of the artist's point of view, and could hardly be considered an objective reflection. Considering what we have discussed about the essence of the artistic, art is necessarily prior to theory – it presages and forms concepts, rather than the other way round. This calls into question whether a study of artistic techniques through analysing past artworks could ever on its own result in a system truly capable of creating original art, which could then be programmed into a computer. As Heidegger argues:

> "The truth that discloses itself in the work can never be proved or derived from what went before. What went before is refuted in its exclusive actuality by the work. What art founds can therefore never be compensated and made up for by what is already at hand and available. Founding is an overflow, a bestowal."[71]

Roger Penrose has attempted to use Gödel's halting theorem to prove we are not computers[72], by showing that some mathematical problems can only be solved from outside the system of all known mathematical knowledge. But artistic creativity causes an even greater difficulty for artificial intelligence development, as it appears to be defined precisely by works which by their very nature transcend existing systems and genres. So what exactly leads so many to think that computers can create art, and could one day even do so of their own accord? Do they just not understand art? In the next chapter, we

---

[70] Friedrich Nietzsche, *The Birth of Tragedy* (New York: Doubleday, 1956), p142

[71] *The origin of the work of art*, in Martin Heidegger, *Basic Writings* (London: Routledge, 1993), p200.

[72] In Roger Penrose, *The Emperor's New Mind* (Oxford: Oxford University Press, 1999) and *Shadows of the Mind* (Oxford: Oxford University Press, 1996).

will look at the origins of traditional computing, and how the faith put in its capability of solving all problems, even those of heuretics[73] and artistic creativity, has its underpinnings firmly in the Western metaphysical tradition.

---

[73] Heuretics, as opposed to hermeneutics, is the logic of invention rather than of interpretation.

Chapter 3
Binary Being

In the previous chapter, we discussed how artistic creativity appears by definition to be in conflict with rule-based action, although the conventional view of art as mimesis has offered the hope of a technological approach. Despite their common heritage in Greek *techne*, art and technology have developed a qualitative difference which has been greatly accentuated in modernity. As Heidegger argues, "Art is history in the essential sense that it grounds history."[74] Modern technology, on the other hand, is a by-product of science and, "Science is not an original happening of truth, but always the cultivation of a domain of truth already opened, specifically by apprehending and confirming that which shows itself to be possibly and necessarily correct within that field."[75] So science and technology are essentially "after the fact", whereas art is much more directly involved in the expression of a directly experienced truth, although it would be puerile to simplify this to a process of "fact production" versus the "fact verification" of science, even if some in the scientific community (and Plato) might see it so. Computers, however, are widely considered to be something rather different from other developments of modern technology, and many predict that they might one day lead to an intelligence akin to our own. Notable amongst these are Ray Kurzweil, as commented upon in the first chapter, Hans Moravec, founder of the world's largest robotics program at Carnegie Mellon University, and MIT's Marvin Minsky. In this chapter, we will discuss where this belief comes from, what the historical and philosophical underpinnings of information technology are in general, and whether there is any possibility that the most prevalent contemporary forms of computing could develop artistic creativity. We will be leaving future forms of computing and their potential for a later chapter.

---

[74] *The origin of the work of art* in Martin Heidegger, *Basic Writings* (London: Routledge, 1993), p202.
[75] _, p187. More succinctly, Heidegger has also argued that "Science does not think."

The an-archaeology of computing[76]

The concept of machine computation is not a new idea. Computing devices can be traced back to increasingly distant origins – Charles Babbage's difference engine, Leonardo da Vinci's programmable Lion robot[77], or even the abacus. Similarly, the theoretical underpinnings of digital computing owe a historical debt to Gottfried Wilhelm von Leibniz's work on the binary structure of culture, George Boole's system of logic, and many others. The modern, digital, electronic device we know today, however, really came into being in the Twentieth Century, as only then did the electronic technology required to implement it become a reality. Historical opinion on who invented the first computer seems almost to depend on the national background of the historian in question. However, it is generally agreed that Konrad Zuse came up with the first freely programmable binary system, the Z1, in Germany in 1936, and finished building it in 1938. Great Britain's Alan Turing, on the other hand, is usually considered the spiritual father of computer science in general, although his computers were still theoretical in 1936. Turing's definition of the Universal Turing Machine[78] remains the theoretical underpinning of computing, although it wasn't until late 1943 that his team finished Colossus. This was another freely programmable computer, famously used to break German Enigma secret codes during the Second World War. The US, from where the majority of 20th Century commercial development has originated, was actually comparatively late on the scene with ENIAC in 1946. The IBM company dates back to the late 1880s, when its precursor was producing dial recorders

[76] Here we will be loosely following a heterogeneous historical method similar to that used by Siegfried Zielinski in *Audiovisions* (Amsterdam: Amsterdam University Press, 1999) and *Deep Time of the Media* (Cambridge, Massachusetts: The MIT Press, 2006). In other words, we will cover a few dead ends as well as the main discoveries in computing which have shaped today's digital systems.
[77] As described in Mark E Rosheim, *Robot Evolution: The Development of Anthrobotics* (New York: John Wiley & Sons Inc, 1994).
[78] The Church-Turing Hypothesis which defines the Universal Turing Machine was developed over a number of academic papers, but the first was A M Turing, "On Computable Numbers, with an Application to the Entscheidungsproblem", *Proceedings of the London Mathematical Society*, series 2, 42 (1936-37), p230-265.

for tracking the hours worked by employees. Herman Hollerith's tabulation machines used in the US census also date back to the 19th century. But neither of these are computers in the modern sense, just information recording devices.

1. Language versus information

Despite the heterogeneous national origins of the computer as a device, the same set of core concepts have dictated the nature of computing in the 20th Century. These have generally followed the model developed in America. One of the most important features that singles out all of these systems from earlier calculation devices such as the IBM dial recorders and tabulation machines is the notion of *free programmability*, first realised in Konrad Zuse's Z1. In most of the early devices named above – with the partial exception of Turing's Colossus, as we will discuss in a later chapter – the computer is considered to be a general-purpose system for calculation, functioning independently of the specific substance of what is being calculated. So long as problems can be abstracted into the general operations used by a computer, the machine can go to work on one problem just as effectively as on any other. But this requirement for abstraction imposes constraints on what computers can do. The initial setup of the process and formulation of the problem ready for solving always needs to be performed by a human operator, although an element of self-teaching has been implemented in some recent systems which can then function more independently once seed parameters have been defined. We'll be discussing the idea of computers learning for themselves and neural net technology later in this chapter. However, even for more advanced contemporary systems, at some point the inconsistency of the real world has to be neatly packaged into neutral "information" for the computer to function successfully. The parameters for this are always predefined by human input. This has been an explicit strategy right from the beginning of modern computing. In his seminal paper on communications theory in 1948, Claude Shannon formulated the issue thus:

"The fundamental problem of communication is that of reproducing at one point either exactly or approximately a message selected at another point. Frequently the messages have *meaning*; that is they refer to or are correlated according to some system with certain physical or conceptual entities. These semantic aspects of communication are irrelevant to the engineering problem. The significant aspect is that the actual message is one *selected from a set* of possible messages. The system must be designed to operate for each possible selection, not just the one which will actually be chosen since this is unknown at the time of design."[79]

This passage could easily be read as a classic example of Heidegger's conception of technology as Enframing. For Shannon, meaning is rendered "irrelevant". Instead, what is important is that a set of possible meanings is predefined, and the system is then exclusively designed to work with these. The system Enframes its possible uses with this predefined set. Shannon's paper has become one of the seminal works of early computer science, and although it is an engineering treatise and not philosophy, it shows how blithely the gamut of human experience is pared back to a "set of possible messages" by communications technology, with the concern for how that set is chosen fundamentally downplayed in importance, or even ignored entirely. This reduction can be seen at work across all the electronic media, but it gains a particular resonance with computers. One of the key features of computers is that they supposedly operate with natural human language. But they first have to reduce that language to a limited code to turn it into an information source in Shannon's conception.

At its most fundamental, this code is considered *binary* in nature. J W Tukey coined the word *bits* from *binary digits* to refer to the minimum unit of information. Although other base counting

---

[79] *A mathematical theory of communications* in Claude E Shannon, *Claude E Shannon: Collected Papers* (New York: John Wiley & Sons Inc, 1993).

systems could have been used, the binary system is considered the simplest. The underlying structure is built entirely on two basic states: on or off, represented by one or zero. It's not the primary purpose of this paper to debate in detail the difference between analog and digital systems, as many of the arguments we will be pursuing could apply equally to an analog computing system as to the predominant digital form. However, the binary system is still an important consideration for the arguments that will be followed regarding specific technologies, so we will outline its development and a few of the problems arising from its use. Binary arithmetic was first developed in the West by Gottfried Wilhelm von Leibniz in the 17th century, and further expanded into a logical system by George Boole in the 19th century. The structuralist movement, taking its lead from Ferdinand de Saussure, found binary oppositions deeply engrained in language, which Levi-Strauss and others extrapolated out into a theory of culture. The classic structuralist ideology holds that although the world may be naturally continuous, the linguistic representation of it in which we all live[80] is essentially structured by oppositions, so it is binary. As a result, the binary cybernetic systems employed by a digital computer are considered ideal for processing human language, and by extension could therefore simulate the workings of culture. However, as Derrida's technique of deconstruction has shown, any dualist assumption has an inherent hierarchy between the two terms in its binary opposition. One term is always the stronger – and some concepts can be two opposing terms at the same time. Derrida's most infamous example of the latter is the notion of Pharmakon[81] found in Plato's *Phaedrus*. The Pharmakon is the poison which is also a cure. We will discuss such "undecidables" further when we look in more detail at the problems faced by artificial intelligence systems in a later chapter. For our purposes so far, it's sufficient here to say that a binary system of opposites is a flawed metaphysical representation of the continuous world, rather than an exact

---

[80] As Hans-Georg Gadamer famously stated in *Truth and Method* (New York: Continuum, 1994), "Being that can be understood is language".
[81] "Plato's pharmacy" in Jacques Derrida, *Dissemination* (New York: Continuum, 2004).

replica. But it's also a very powerful and effective representation. As Nietzsche argued long before the advent of computers, the false can be beneficial for human survival, or even something necessary for it. Binarism has also shown itself capable of reproducing the world with enough fidelity for the vast majority of people to believe in the copy, and for simulations to derive results which conform very accurately to the real world. The average music buyer would generally agree that the music CD produces better quality sound than the LP record. But there will always be something missed out – the example which doesn't fit either pole of the opposition. As such, the post-structuralist critique of dualist structuralism has severe implications for traditional binary computing.

But Shannon's theory of communications, as touched upon earlier, isn't fundamentally tied to binarism. What it does do is set up a rigid view of communications from an engineering perspective, with an information source, transmitter, channel, receiver, and destination – something which is mirrored in computing to this day. For Shannon, communication in general is roughly divided into discrete, continuous and mixed types – for example, telegraphy (a string of single letters), radio (eg music broadcasts), and PCM speech encoding respectively, where "a discrete channel will mean a system whereby a sequence of choices from a finite set of symbols $S_1,..., S_n$ can be transmitted from one point to another"[82]. Shannon's theories primarily deal with discrete communication. Considering the information source, he argues that "the main point at issue is the effect of statistical knowledge about the source in reducing the required capacity of the channel, by use of proper encoding of the information."[83] The sequences of letters in telegraphy "are not completely random. In general, they form sentences and have the statistical structure of, say, English."[84] How these statistics of language usage are derived is fundamentally important – the statistics of English as used in Oxford in the UK

[82] A mathematical theory of communications, in Claude E Shannon, Claude E Shannon: Collected Papers (New York: John Wiley & Sons Inc, 1993).
[83] ___.
[84] ___.

are likely to be somewhat different to those of the dialect of English used in Jamaica. There will, of course, be many similarities, otherwise understanding between Oxford inhabitants and Jamaicans would be impossible. Although it is sometimes difficult for people speaking different dialects of the same language to comprehend each other, it's not usually impossible. But it's also clear that a system devised to convey one language efficiently will be less efficient for another. Indeed, at the time of writing voice recognition software had to be programmed with different databases depending on the dialect of the speaker. Ideographical languages have proven even more problematic for computer interfaces devised in the West, which are optimised for the more limited character set of alphanumerical text. Codification into computer-friendly information risks far greater alteration of meaning than merely translating from one language to another, and even the latter has its inherent problems[85].

The statistical model of language used by Shannon presents a stochastic system of probabilities that one letter will follow another. Aside from the assumptions about which dialect of a language is used, the assumption is also that the statistical values are static. Historical changes in language usage are downplayed. Shannon shows how a statistical model allied with a random number series generates something vaguely like human speech. He goes on to add "it appears then that a sufficiently complex stochastic process will give a satisfactory representation of a discrete source."[86] Since Shannon's time of writing, similar stochastic processes have been used to provide the automatic spelling correction found in word processors or the text prediction in mobile phones, both of which are generally considered to be useful enhancements. However, Shannon already hints at a potential problem with such a system of probabilities which arises when two choices are equally

---

[85] Umberto Eco's *Mouse or Rat? Translation as negotiation* (London: Weidenfeld & Nicolson, 2003) discusses these problems in detail, in particular the Italian language's lack of distinction between mice or rats in common parlance when using the word "topo".
[86] *A mathematical theory of communications*, in Claude E Shannon, *Claude E Shannon: Collected Papers* (New York: John Wiley & Sons Inc, 1993).

probable.[87] He introduces a concept of uncertainty, which he uses the letter H to represent. An 'H' value of one is totally uncertain, whereas zero means totally certain. Computing methods gain no advantage in an environment of total uncertainty. However, Shannon argues that human language is somewhere in between the two, and introduces the notion of redundancy to illustrate this:

> "The redundancy of ordinary English, not considering statistical structure over greater distances than about eight letters, is roughly 50 per cent. This means that when we write English half of what we write is determined by the structure of the language and half is chosen freely. The figure 50 per cent was found by several independent methods which all gave results in this neighbourhood."[88]

This notion of redundancy is based on how many letters can be deleted and still maintain meaning. It's linked to uncertainty, in the sense that the more uncertainty there is, the less redundancy. Shannon actually goes so far as to relate this to language used to express artistic sentiments, comparing such language to more utilitarian discourse:

> "Two extremes of redundancy in English prose are represented by Basic English and by James Joyce's book 'Finnegans Wake'. The Basic English vocabulary is limited to 850 words and the redundancy is very high. This is reflected in the expansion that occurs when a passage is translated into Basic English. Joyce on the other hand enlarges the vocabulary and

---

[87] "Suppose we have a set of possible events whose probabilities of occurrence are p1, p2..., pn. These probabilities are known but that is all we know concerning which event will occur. Can we find a measure of how much 'choice' is involved in the selection of the event or how uncertain we are of the outcome?" And: "With equally likely events there is more choice, or uncertainty, when there are more possible events." ___.

[88] ____, p14-15

is alleged to achieve a compression of
semantic content."[89]

Hidden behind Shannon's Joyce example is the assumption that
"Basic English" and the language of experimental literature are
intending to achieve the same goal – namely communicating a
specific message or piece of information from A to B. This is not
a neutral assumption, because artistic messages in particular are
difficult to decompose into discrete units of information. As we
discussed in the last chapter, the meaning of an artwork is often
not clearly defined by the person creating it, and is instead
developed later by those perceiving it. Artworks certainly don't
fit into the definition described earlier where units of
information are singled out from a possible set of messages. A
sentence from Joyce is not one possibility from a finite set of
possibilities, but in fact gains its importance as literature from
the fact that it breaks with existing traditions, finding new
possibilities. So it isn't part of a traditional set of possibilities at
all. In fact, as Umberto Eco has argued[90], the punning in
Finnegans Wake makes it more a vehicle for the reader to find
their own significance than a message with a fixed meaning. The
artistic message cannot be allotted a probability, and so
statements like, "the messages of high probability are
represented by short codes and those of low probability by long
codes"[91], simply cannot be applied to artistic language.
However, at another level Shannon is expressing something
which does ring true in a more general sense – that highly
original and creative work is extremely singular, and therefore
difficult to communicate other than in its original form. In a
sense, the "it happens" in art discussed in the previous chapter
pushes it into a realm which the mathematics of communications
underpinning computing is not designed to cope with. Lyotard
argues along similar lines:

---

[89] _____, p15
[90] Umberto Eco, *The Role of the Reader* (Bloomington: Indiana University Press,
1979).
[91] *A mathematical theory of communications*, in Claude E Shannon, *Claude E
Shannon: Collected Papers* (New York: John Wiley & Sons Inc, 1993), p17

"[the seduction of the art market] exerts itself thanks to a confusion between innovation and the *Ereignis*, a confusion maintained by the temporality specific to contemporary capitalism. 'Strong' information, if one can call it that, exists in inverse proportion to the meaning that can be attributed to it in the code available to its receiver. It is like 'noise'. It is easy for the public and for artists, advised by intermediaries – the diffusers of cultural merchandise – to draw from this observation the principle that a work of art is avant-garde in direct proportion to the extent that it is stripped of meaning. Is it not then like an event?"[92]

There is yet another assumption in part of Shannon's theory. This holds that for some messages (at least theoretically) only one interpretation is possible. In the language of engineering it's stated thus: "If a source can produce only one particular message its entropy is zero, and no channel is required."[93] This assumption leads to methods of dealing with situations where the message doesn't necessarily get through without loss:

"If the channel is noisy it is not in general possible to reconstruct the original message of the transmitted signal with *certainty* by any operation on the received signal *E*. There are, however, ways of transmitting the information which are optimal in combating noise."[94]

To optimise the communication, the noisy system is calibrated by an observer who can read the original message without noise and see how it is being received, again without noise, and then work out how to compensate. However, Shannon discusses this

---

[92] *The Inhuman*, Jean Francois Lyotard, p106
[93] *A mathematical theory of communications*, in Claude E Shannon, *Claude E Shannon: Collected Papers* (New York: John Wiley & Sons Inc, 1993), p18
[94] _____, p20

from the perspective of the "noiseless case"[95]. Using the resulting error correction, computers are considered to be able to output a message close enough to the input to be useful. But noise is a fact of life – all linguistic communication is effected by noise, and understanding is never perfect. This is a classic case of how scientific discourse disregards the inherent bias of the observer, at least up to Einstein and Heisenberg (of which more later). The godlike objective abstraction of the Newtonian physical paradigm has been carried through to computing and the age of information.

2. Sequential versus parallel

Another key characteristic of the modern computer is the sequential way it deals with its tasks. Originally laid out in *First Draft of a Report on the EDVAC* in 1945, John von Neumann's design for the EDVAC computer system set up the architecture for all subsequent computers: a single CPU accesses a memory system that holds both program and data. This foreclosed a vastly different line of development that Alan Turing was pursuing in Manchester, which assumed massive parallelism. We'll be discussing some of Turing's other contributions later in this chapter. As with Shannon's communications theory, Von Neumann's automatic computing system required that "the instructions which govern this operation must be given to the device in absolutely exhaustive detail", and "all these procedures require the use of some code, to express the logical and the algebraical definition of the problem under consideration, as well as the necessary numerical material"[96]. In other words, the input data is converted into information which the device can understand by the programmer – the device itself does not engage in the process of encoding information.

---

[95] Contrast this with Kant's notion of artistic communication without language (see previous chapter).
[96] John Von Neumann, *First Draft of a Report on the EDVAC* (communicated between the United States Army Ordnance Department and the University of Pennsylvania Moore School of Electrical Engineering University of Pennsylvania, 1945), §1.2.

Von Neumann defined an algorithmic computing style that is highly unsuitable for cognitive tasks like pattern recognition or "thinking", as each stage of computation involves a linear process of reading code and data, operating upon it, and writing it back. This breaks down operations into independent chunks. However, at the time he considered his computational model to be analogous to the human brain: "The three specific parts CA, CC (together C) and M correspond to the *associative* neurons in the human nervous system. It remains to discuss the equivalents of the *sensory* or *afferent* and the *motor* or *efferent* neurons. These are the *input* and the *output* organs of the device".[97] Figure 1 below gives a pictorial representation of the Von Neumann architecture.

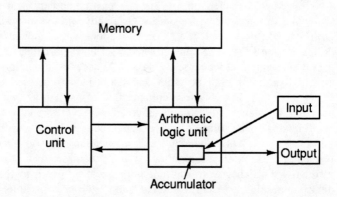

Figure 1 – Schematic of the Von Neumann computer architecture, with input/output, central control, arithmetical unit and memory

However, Von Neumann describes a neuron as existing in states of equilibrium, "two or more distinct states in which it can exist indefinitely." This model has dictated the way computer memory is designed right up to the present day. But neurological research has long since shown that the human brain is a much more

---

[97] ___, §2.6. CA is the central arithmetical part, CC the central control and M the memory.

complicated network of interrelated influences than a collection of on/off switches. So, when Von Neumann states: "It is worth mentioning that the neurons of the higher animals are definitely elements in the above sense. They have an all-or-none character, that is two states: Quiescent and excited", he is working with a model of the human mind which has been superseded, although he was of course bound by the development of neuroscience contemporary to him (the 1940s). Still, this conception of how neurons work was translated into the electronics of computing[98], and remains dominant to this day. The two states of equilibrium "suggest the use of the binary system"[99], which is now the native language of computers. Most importantly, however, Von Neumann made computers strictly non-parallel in operation: "The device should be as simple as possible, that is, contain as few elements as possible. This can be achieved by never performing two operations simultaneously, if this would cause a significant increase in the number of elements required." As the human brain in fact operates in a massively parallel fashion, the Von Neumann model has pushed computers in a very different direction to neuroscience's discoveries of how brains function. Neuroscience currently calculates that human neurons cycle around 200 times a second, but billions of them are running in parallel. Modern computer chips, in contrast, calculate just a couple of instructions at once, but cycle a few billion times a second.

Of course, there are alternatives to the Von Neumann architecture, and some of them have even been encoded into software, although most of this has stalled at the experimental and research stages. Alonzo Church's 1941 thesis *The Calculi of Lambda Conversion* described a new algebra of recursive functions, which was eventually taken up by John McCarthy[100] for his definition of the LISP programming language. Recursive

---

[98] "It is easily seen that these simplified neuron functions can be imitated by telegraph relays or by vacuum tubes." ___, §4.2.
[99] ___, §5.1.
[100] John McCarthy, "Recursive Functions of Symbolic Expressions and their Computation by Machine" *Communications of the ACM*, 3 (April 1960), p184-195.

functions process symbols rather than numbers, which would be crucial to any real advance toward intelligent machines[101]. Jim Backus, inventor of the conventional Fortran programming language, also used a more mild version of recursive functions to argue against the von Neumann computing method[102]. Backus devised a new "functional programming" (FP) style, which doesn't involve a repetitive reading and writing of small units to a memory store. Instead, FP builds the computing program into a large algebraic function of interconnected operations, which execute in one motion. This has spawned a number of attempts to escape the Von Neumann tradition. But they have all remained obscure and underdeveloped because they were orders of magnitudes slower than the conventional C or Fortran languages at everyday business calculations. This limited the use of lambda calculus or FP computing for commercial data processing, and hence rendered them unattractive for large-scale funding and development. Even though the processors available at the beginning of the 21st century are finally fast enough to run programs based on recursive functions at useful speeds, the traditional method has become dominant, so contemporary computing as monopolised by companies like Microsoft has educated generations of software engineers that imperative, C language-style programming is the only way. Hence, the von Neumann computer has a virtually complete dominance over a more symbolic approach that doesn't suffer from the tight structure required by sequential computing. However, recursive functions are seen by some as one of the answers to the problem of creating intelligent machines[103]. An example recursive structure is shown in Figure 2.

---

[101] To underline this potential, Harold Cohen claims the huge leaps forward in his Aaron painting system can be credited to his switch in the early 1990s to using LISP as the programming language.

[102] Jim Backus, "Can Programming be Liberated from the Von Neumann Style?", *Communications of the ACM*, Volume 21 issue 8 (August 1978).

[103] In particular, Ray Kurzweil has suggested the use of recursive functions in *The Age of Spiritual Machines* (London: Texere, 2001).

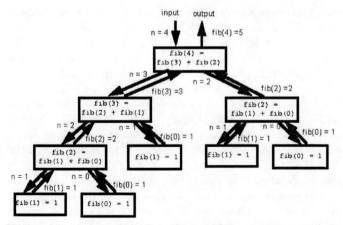

Figure 2 – A recursive function, which executes a whole series of interconnected operations in one process

Linked to the idea of using software that deals with symbols rather than numbers, it is also possible to conceive of computing using parallel rather than sequential processing. D Rumelhart and J McLelland's 1986 *Parallel distributed processing* and Tuevo Kohonen's 1977 *Associative memory: a system-theoretical approach* set out the principles of modern neural network computing, an alternative to von Neumann-style algorithmic processing. This connectionist approach has proven itself much more successful at pattern recognition and cognitive problems. However, although neural nets have found applications in military circles, as with the recursive functions described above they have been held back because they are not much good for everyday commercial data processing. This has meant that neural net processing hasn't been encoded into silicon-based hardware in the same way that Von Neumann machines have been integrated by the likes of Intel and Motorola. It's also worth noting that the parallel computing which does exist today is essentially made up of a collection of von Neumann computers which still function independently from each other, as well as operating on chunks of data in a sequence.

Alongside parallelism, neural nets use feedback loops between processing layers to set up their computational relationships between input data and output results. Since human brains also use feedback loops between neurons, this has also been cited as another example of how neural nets are closer to the functioning of consciousness. However, most neural nets only have one or two layers between the input and output levels, and the feedback schematics are relatively simple. The human brain's neo-cortex has six layers, each one massively interconnected with others, and with hugely complicated feedback loops between them. Neural nets also require training with sample data, for which the results are already known. They are then adjusted to give the correct results. This learning process only occurs during setup, after which the neural net is essentially static. This again is entirely unlike the human brain, which is able to develop through its entire lifespan. Figure 3 shows an example schematic for a simple neural net.

In contrast, the conventional approach to programming which has developed to complement the Von Neumann approach to processing essentially revolves around an object-oriented paradigm. This idea, first introduced by O-J Dahl and B Myrhaug in their 1969 paper *SIMULA 67 Implementation Guide*, is found behind all the popular languages used at the time of writing - Visual Basic, C++, C#, and Java amongst others. Object-oriented programs break software into components called objects, which consist of variables and associated methods for controlling them. These components are intended to be modular – each one can be developed independently and has a set interface for communicating with other objects. While this method has helped develop programming as a business venture by breaking software down into manageable chunks, here again the resemblance to how the human brain works is tenuous at best. Where programming objects function discretely, the various parts of the brain affect each other's workings at a very low level, via exceedingly complex feedback loops. Object-oriented programming also presents another example of Heidegger's Enframing technology at work. Although objects can be combined together to perform a wide variety of very different tasks, many of which weren't intended by their original programmers, they still dictate what can and cannot be done with computers. Software objects generally have a clearly defined purpose and mode of operation, reducing the likelihood that that they will achieve anything other than what was intended. They therefore are not well suited for creating a machine which can think creatively for itself. The most extreme object-oriented software is called "black box programming", which treats objects entirely as opaque units where only the input and output behaviour are deemed important. What's going on inside is considered entirely irrelevant.

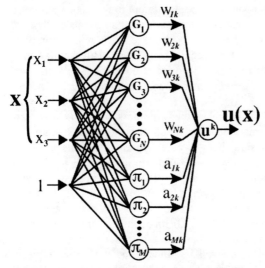

Figure 3 – The schematic for a neural net processing system.

In summary, apart from a few specialised exceptions, the predominant type of computer system at the beginning of the 21st century still processes independent software chunks sequentially. Operations are executed one at a time. Even when more than one operation is performed at once, this is merely used as a way to speed up the processing of an essentially linear calculation. This is to be contrasted to a scenario where an operation consists of a host of functions executing in parallel, which affect each other in a non-sequential fashion. We will be discussing in later chapters whether a parallel computing of this type could lead to devices capable of creating art, as some computer scientists such as Ray Kurzweil believe. However, even these devices are likely to have another obstacle to circumvent, namely that they operate using a simulated model of the world.

3. Computer simulation

One of the major uses of computing for decades has been simulation. Computer games try to resemble reality in a 3D-animated world, scientific models attempt to replicate real-world processes so as to predict outcomes, and the now-jaded "virtual reality" valiantly endeavours to immerse the user in a complete visual replacement of a spatial environment. But simulation is more than just one application of computer technology amongst many others. By their very nature, computers process an abstract simulated model of the world, rather than working directly on the world itself. This makes them quintessentially postmodern. They are the ultimate materialisation of Baudrillard's simulacra, and the world inside them is pure hyperreality. This tendency towards virtualisation was ingrained into information technology from the beginning. Alan Turing's famous Turing Test defined the information technology age by suggesting that the best way to test if a computer could think was to see if its answers to various questions could be distinguished from real human answers given by another human.[104] In other words, what acts like a human might as well be human, and the virtual replaces the actual. This is the premise of many works of science fiction,

---

[104] "The new form of the problem can be described in terms of a game which we call the 'imitation game'. It is played with three people a man (A), a woman (B), and an interrogator (C) who may be of either sex. The interrogator stays in a room apart front the other two. The object of the game for the interrogator is to determine which of the other two is the man and which is the woman. He knows them by labels X and Y, and at the end of the game he says either 'X is A and Y is B' or 'X is B and Y is A.' The interrogator is allowed to put questions to A and B. We now ask the question, 'What will happen when a machine takes the part of A in this game?' Will the interrogator decide wrongly as often when the game is played like this as he does when the game is played between a man and a woman? These questions replace our original, 'Can machines think?'" Alan Turing, "Computing machinery and intelligence", *Mind 49* (1950), p433-460.

most famously Philip K. Dick's *Do androids dream of electric sheep?*[105], which was made into the highly successful film *Bladerunner* by Ridley Scott in 1982.

The tendency towards the virtual in computing is also derived from its basis in information theory. As discussed earlier in the chapter during the analysis of Shannon's engineering treatise and the von Neumann computing style, computers require the world to be reduced to information, and for that information to be binary in nature. This leads them to exist in a virtual world, as they function at least one step removed from direct experience, in a purely symbolic realm. However, the Turing test questions whether this does in fact prevent computers from appearing human. The notion that human thinking is itself binary has been discredited for some time, since the post-structuralist critique developed. But that wouldn't necessarily prevent a binary system from passing the Turing Test, which doesn't really care what's "under the bonnet". After all, no human knows exactly what another human is thinking anyway. This is the fundamental problem of Qualia, which we touched upon right at the beginning in Chapter 1 (see p9) – a key focus in the artificial intelligence debate.

Simulation has become a major fascination for postmodernism. As Derrida argues:

> "A perfect imitation is no longer an imitation. If one eliminates the tiny difference that, in separating the imitator from the imitated, by that very fact refers to it, one would render the imitator absolutely different: the imitator would become another being no longer referring to the imitated."[106]

Derrida's fascination with iteration and identity, as evidenced here, will be discussed in the next chapter in the context of

---

[105] Philip K. Dick, *Do androids dream of electric sheep?* (New York: Doubleday, 1968).

[106] Jacques Derrida, *Dissemination* (New York: Continuum, 2004), p138-9.

subjectivity. However, the difference between something being "like" something else and actually being that something is already crucial for this strand of the argument. If computers merely pass the Turing test, they can't necessarily create true art, they just make something that looks sufficiently like it to convince people. This brings us back to the concept of mimesis discussed in the last chapter. If art is merely a mirror, then computer technology could conceivably create art merely by mirroring the world. But any media device since the photographic camera can already do that, albeit with the help of a human operator. Merely taking a photo does not create art. There is still a special skill in taking a *good* photo. As we have already argued, art has a presentational element that is not mimetic in nature, and this is what an art-creating computational device must also perform. Simple mirroring is not enough.

Resemblance is a distinct problem for computers, which as we discussed earlier presuppose that a single symbol has a single meaning. Homonyms and homophones, another of Derrida's favourite topics[107], pose distinct difficulties for computerised tasks like voice recognition. The meaning of a word is usually ascertained by referencing contextual information, such as the rest of the sentence containing the problematic word. However, poetry often deliberately plays on the multiple levels of meaning in homonyms and homophones. Sometimes these poetic word games offer no clearly defined primary meaning, and more than one could be possible. The semantic resonance is allowed to play well beyond the everyday semantic content of the poetic phrase. This is also true of allegorical language found in many types of drama – the German Mourning Play is singled out for example by Samuel Weber.[108] In all these examples, the many levels of meaning are all important, and indeed part of the artistry of the work. To focus on one and discard the others is to miss the point

---

[107] See Gregory L Ulmer, *Applied Grammatology* (Baltimore and London: The Johns Hopkins University Press, 1985) for a detailed discussion of homonymy and homophony in Derrida's opus.
[108] Samuel Weber, "Genealogy of Modernity: History, Myth and Allegory in Benjamin's *Origin of the German Mourning Play*", *MLN*, Vol 106, No 3, German Issue (April 1991), p465-500.

entirely. Indeed, "taking things literally" is often cited as a form of stupidity. By this yardstick, mono-semantic "intelligent" computing systems would be the stupidest beings of all.

But most problematic of all for computers is the process of *catechresis* discussed by Ulmer, again with reference to Derrida[109]. In the process of *catechresis*, the poeisis in philosophy uses a kind of metaphorical language where a word takes on a new meaning to describe a concept previously without linguistic representation. Ulmer uses Heidegger's example from Plato, where the word *eidos* is coined to refer to the underlying structure or *hypokeimenon*. Previously, *eidos* had meant outward appearance. *Catechresis* is a common process in all theory, from philosophy to theoretical physics. For example, we will be discussing Deleuze's catechretic reworking of the notion of folding in a later chapter. The fluidity of meanings exemplified by homonyms and homophones is a fundamental part of being human. The implied lack of a direct connection between the world as it appears in our imagination and the world as it actually is (or between beings and Being) is a necessary element of life. As Zizek argues:

> "...for Kant, direct access to the noumenal domain would deprive us of the very 'spontaneity' that forms the core of transcendental freedom: it would turn us into lifeless automata or, to put it in today's terms, into computers, into 'thinking machines'."[110]

This is precisely what some artificial intelligence researches actually argue.[111] In all the discussions of virtual reality and simulation, however, a simple fact is often downplayed – that the reality which is being mimicked is necessarily prior to the

---

[109] Gregory L Ulmer, *Applied Grammatology* (Baltimore and London: The Johns Hopkins University Press, 1985).

[110] Slavoj Zizek, *The Ticklish Subject* (London: Verso, 1999), p60.

[111] For example, in *Consciousness Explained* (London: Penguin, 1993), Daniel Dennett claims that subjective experience is a mythological side effect of our mechanical brains. He therefore denies the existence of Qualia entirely.

mimicry.[112] This is not a chicken and egg scenario. For something to be virtually real, the real must have come first. Without this, the simulation is pure imagination, which is a solipsistic stance that has indeed been argued by some philosophical traditions, and more than one major world religion. But few would argue in its favour in the modern world. In the case of computerised simulation, it is not so much how close to reality the simulation is, but what it adds to that reality by simultaneously referring to it and to something which has never *really* existed. The 3D animation used in film-making and computer games, for example, is generally used to extend our experiences rather than just fake existing ones. Few explosions are ever quite as large as they are in the movies.

The ultimate Enframing tool

From the theoretical works of computer science discussed in this chapter, it becomes clear that the computer is a classic example of instrumental technology as described by Heidegger in *The question concerning technology*. To express this in Heidegger's own terminology, the computer represents certain human brain faculties transformed into a standing reserve. However, although the computer is widely thought to be modelled on the human brain, in fact it only models a small subset of human mental faculties. It uses binary systems to perform a very limited set of algorithmic functions. To turn this around, and impute human intelligence to computers, would be to allow our sense of what we are to become Enframed (as Heidegger would have put it) by our own technology. The all-pervasive digitalisation of our culture is dictating what we can do with our existence as human beings. Lyotard's statement that "Technology wasn't invented by us humans. Rather the other way round"[113] is even more true

---

[112] "...the thing imitated is before the imitation. [] However often this order may be reversed throughout history, the absolute discernibility between the imitated and the imitation, and the anteriority of the former over the latter, have never been displaced." Gregory Ulmer, *Applied grammatology* (Baltimore and London: The Johns Hopkins University Press, 1985), p177.

[113] Jean-Francois Lyotard, *The Inhuman* (Stanford: Stanford University Press, 1991), p12.

of computer culture than for the technical developments that went before. The computer supposedly liberates us all to be artists in our own homes, but in fact the options are limited and we're just being cloned by media (as Schirmacher argues[114]), only more subtly than in previous eras. Sherry Turkle calls computers the latest "object to think with"[115], yet those who do so in an uncritical way would be limiting their horizons of existence to that of a glorified pocket calculator.

As already discussed, Shannon's seminal work *A mathematical theory of communication* shows that the definition of information used in mainstream IT has great limitations as a general-purpose method for delineating human experience into discrete units. Bits and bytes are treated as neutral in information theory, whereas some bits are far more valuable to humans than others. Art, in particular, shows the limitation of the notion of information. To be information at all, something needs to be clearly and exhaustively defined as part of a set, missing the ambiguous revealing/concealing of truth as *aletheia* in art. When language is transformed into bits and bytes, it becomes standing reserve, rather than an organic human development. Information technology transmits facts, which are a reduced subset of truth. If truth itself is not clear, as with the examples of homonyms and homophones, or Derrida's undecidables such as the Pharmakon, then the transmission of facts becomes problematic. Walter Benjamin's notion of "aura" represents the awe-inspiring singularity encountered traditional art. So is mechanical reproduction without singularity and therefore artless? This doesn't appear to be true, considering the body of digitally derived works which are now internationally acclaimed as new media art. But digital technology does take mechanical reproduction to an effortless extreme, further hiding the singularity of art, despite the fact that this singularity is what delineates the individual human existence. For a computer to make art, it must incorporate the singularity of the human

---

[114] Wolfgang Schirmacher, *Cloning Humans with Media: Impermanence and Imperceptible Perfection*, http://www.egs.edu/faculty/schirmacher/schirmacher-cloning-humans-with-media.html (2000).
[115] Sherry Turkle, *Life on the Screen* (New York: Touchstone, 1995).

individual. In the next chapter, we will analyse what a human individual actually is, compared to the computer device, before moving on to imagine what an artificial intelligence might need to incorporate in order to become a truly creative being.

Chapter 4
Changing the subject

In the last two chapters, we discussed how artistic works express life experience, without having to be directly derived from the materiality of *what* is happening. Computers, in contrast, were defined as general-purpose devices for operating on pre-packaged information. They function using symbols representing clearly (pre)defined objects. What separates the two most of all, however, is how they relate to humans as individuals. Art communicates in a physical and emotional way through individuals, who are its creators and perceivers. Aesthetics is therefore a highly subjective experience, perhaps the most subjective of all. So it loses its relevance entirely when de-contextualised from the artist and audience. On the other hand, we have argued that computers are a product of instrumental technology as critiqued by Heidegger[116], so they are created with a specific purpose in mind. This dictates how they are meant to be used irregardless of the user or context. Even though computers are intended to be general-purpose "universal" calculating machines, which we discussed in the previous chapter, the range of possible uses for them is circumscribed by how they work. They are essentially algorithmic calculators, and their application is dictated by their sequential processing of software broken into discrete, supposedly independent chunks of code. Art comes into being at the point where an individual encounters the world, and is therefore a different experience for each person. "The sublime feeling is neither moral universality nor aesthetic universalization, but is, rather, the destruction of one by the other in the violence of their differend. This differend cannot demand, even subjectively, to be communicated to all thought." [117] But the computer is part of the human technological programme to dominate the world and dictate experiences, recasting the world in mankind's image of itself. If art is indeed

---

[116] Heidegger's most famous critique of instrumental technology can be found in *The Question Concerning Technology* (New York: Harper Torchbooks, 1977).
[117] Jean-Francois Lyotard, *Lessons on the Analytic of the Sublime* (Stanford: Stanford University Press, 1994), p239.

all about expressing the encounter between humanity and its culturally mediated environment, computer technology faces a problem. How could a device intended to produce consistently the same outcome from a given input ever be part of such a personal, singular, unpredictable encounter as that found in art – since the computer's result must be defined in advance algorithmically?

To answer this question, we need to analyse what constitutes an individual human subject in greater depth. From this process, we would hope to realise more clearly how the role of individuality differs when encountering art compared to using a computer. The conception of the subject must necessarily be at the crux of any debate regarding the possibility of computer creativity, or indeed the possibility of any artificial intelligence, artistically creative or otherwise. The field of artificial intelligence will be covered in more detail in the next chapter, relating it to past research into the field. But before we can move onto this technological side of the discussion, we need to take a more historical and conceptual perspective on subjectivity and identity. Consciousness of self is one of the main characteristics put forward to separate mankind from animals and other beings. Its development is considered one of the most important phases of a child's maturation[118]. However, identity still remains a mysterious idea, which has progressed through numerous guises over the last few millennia of Western thought. When the debate focuses on technological devices such as computers, the most telling argument surrounds whether or not human identity and consciousness can be separated from human corporeality and integrated into an artificial device. If it can't, then no computing system could hope to exhibit fully human intelligence unless it is exactly like a human in every physical respect. But where does the notion that a person can be separated from his or her body come from in the first place? As we will see, this metaphysical debate is not just a problem for computer science, but has an important implication for Western culture in general.

---

[118] Lacan traces this initial phase of self-consciousness via his conception of the Mirror Stage, where an infant aged 6-18 months comes to terms with its reflection in a mirror being both itself and not itself.

A brief history of 'me'

The modern conception of selfhood has not always existed. In fact, the notion of self has developed throughout human history. Many would argue that what we call a self today had not yet been fully formed in the Middle Ages or in Antiquity. It could also be argued that what we call a self in the West does not find an exact parallel in cultures which do not share our Graeco-Roman and Judeo-Christian heritages. Indeed, the words used in contemporary language to refer to identity encode the history of the conception of Western subjectivity within their changing meanings. Even a brief glance at the etymology of the primary terms can reveal some important insights.

"Personality", for example, comes from the Latin *per sona*, meaning "that which the sound comes through". It originally referred to a mask incorporating a built-in funnel for amplifying the voice, which was worn by Roman or Greek actors. This mask was also decorated to convey the role the actor was playing. Taken in the context of its historical foundation, the word "personality" refers to a point of origin for the spoken word, but also a deliberately chosen face which is presented to the social world. Even two millennia ago, therefore, there was the nucleus of a personal identity which was externalised and objectified into a mask that could be consciously fashioned or even swapped for another, alternative mask. It was also the point of origination for primary acts of communication. Today, personality is where the individual meets the social.

The word "subject", on the other hand, is now used as a technical term to refer to the self in social science and philosophy. But it comes from the Latin *subiectum*, meaning "put down or put under". This is essentially a Roman translation of the Greek *hypokeimenon*, a term frequently meditated upon by philosophers from Aristotle to Heidegger and beyond. In both Latin and Greek cases, the subject is what is laid out before the observer – again a physical externalisation, although with other implications to which we will be returning later, when turn our attention to discussing the cognitive functions of subjectivity.

Both *subiectum* and *hypokeimenon* reveal cultures that had not yet developed some of the important nuances of the modern conception of self. As Heidegger argues with regards to *hypokeimenon*:

> "The word names that-which-lies-before, which, as ground, gathers everything onto itself. This metaphysical meaning of the concept of subject has first of all no special relationship to man – and none at all to the I."[119]

However, a change does occur when man becomes the primary *subiectum*: "Man becomes the relational center of that which is as such."[120] In medieval times, Being stands before God – God is the focal point of the *subiectum*, which is therefore still not equated with man alone. But the modern conception places man at the centre, and is even further from the original Greek *hypokeimenon*. This becomes clear if we recall Parmenides' famous dictum that "Thinking and being are the same thing." [121] As Heidegger explains regarding the Greek era, "That which is does not come into being at all through the fact that man first looks upon it... Rather, man is the one who is looked upon by that which is."[122] In other words, being works through man rather than gaining its existence as a product of his subjective view. Heidegger argues in *The age of the world picture*[123] that the end result of this change in the nuance of *subiectum* is Plato's conception of *eidos*. This becomes the seed that grows into our current conception of the world as represented image, because it uses a word for visible form to coin an expression for the underlying ideal form behind material objects.

---

[119] Martin Heidegger, *The Question Concerning Technology* (New York: Harper Torchbooks, 1977), p128.

[120] _____, p128.

[121] Parmenides fragment, quoted from Karl Jaspers, *The Great Philosophers, Volume II: Anaximander, Heraclitus, Parmenides, Plotinus, Lao-Tzu, Nagarjuna* (New York and London: Harvest, 1966), p21.

[122] Martin Heidegger, *The Question Concerning Technology* (New York: Harper Torchbooks, 1977), p131.

[123] _____, p115-154.

But the word "individual" itself is perhaps the most topical term
in any discussion of human subjectivity, considering the Western
capitalist emphasis on individuality as a primary goal of
existence. The Latin origin means something which cannot be
divided – a singularity, much as we earlier defined the art-event
in Chapter 2. For incumbent capitalist culture, the individual is
the smallest unit in the economic enterprise. However, as
Deleuze and Guattari have argued[124], the human individual is far
from being indivisible. In a modern world where change and
adapting to circumstances are the norm, they argue that perhaps
"dividual" is more appropriate. Differentiation has become the
primary subjective motivation, leading to multiple selves, each
one depending on the context. Habit makes us repeat similar
characteristics in different contexts, but life's many surprises
always drag us forward to form new and unique habits for
various environments. In this way, each new situation allows
development of a new persona to fit the occasion – our
subjectivity evolves with our choices and experience.

However, in order to differentiate, you must first have an
understanding of what is identical. As Heidegger argues in
Identity and difference[125], identity is a fundamental term without
which much of human endeavour, in particular science, would
be impossible. In the absence of identity, no object could be
identified to corroborate a scientific theory. The commonly held
conception of identity is one of *equality* – in other words "A =
A". However, Heidegger argues that this should at least be
reformulated "A is A", where something is considered to be the
same as itself, not equal to another example of itself. "Two are
not needed, as they are in the case of equality."[126] But, in fact,
the commonly held conception of identity as equality reveals a
great deal about the status of identity as an *iteration*, or an
example of Nietzsche's Eternal Recurrence of the Same (which
Fred Ulfers has tellingly translated as the Eternal Recurrence of

[124] Gille Deleuze and Felix Guattari, *Anti-Oedipus* (New York: Continuum, 2004).
[125] Martin Heidegger, *Identity and Difference* (Chicago and London: The University of Chicago Press, 1969).
[126] _____, p24.

the *Similar*[127] rather than the same). Without identity, there can be no repetition, for nothing would ever be the same to repeat.

The conception of identity as equality is therefore a primary feature of human cognition. When a feature of the world at hand is recognised, its identity is confirmed – in other words, it is singled out as an iteration of an object-concept. Wittgenstein, however, realised that this can no longer be viewed as the direct correlation between an ideal conception and an experienced object which is just one more example of that conception[128]. He argued that no core set of characteristics can be found for an object's identity, and instead offered "family resemblances" between objects considered to be members of the same conceptual group. In fact, for Wittgenstein the ideal conception is essentially an empty, unattainable thing – something fumbled for in the similarities between objects of a given type, rather than clearly delineated from mind to matter[129]. Identity *as a human construct* is what brings beings and Being together. In the traditional view of identity as equality, identity is a characteristic of Being – Being comes first. Now that belief in God has subsided, an ideal mathematical world has taken its place, but the basic conceptual structure remains the same. In Heidegger's reformulation in *Identity and Difference*, however, Being comes after identity and is a characteristic of it. Reconciling this with Wittgenstein's thinking, concepts do not start off as disembodied mental ideals looking for their equal match in everyday experience. Instead, they are built out of the encounter between the world and our active power to conceptualise the structure we find in the social world. Studies of how children acquire speech have shown clear corroboration of this theory with regards to language[130]. At a certain age, children exhibit an innate ability not only to absorb the language around them, but actually to construct grammatical relationships, even where none existed

---

[127] Friedrich Ulfers, in seminary discussion at the European Graduate School.

[128] Ludwig Wittgenstein, *Philosophical Investigations* (Oxford: Blackwell, 2001).

[129] As will be explained later in this chapter, Wittgenstein's philosophy has found extensive corroboration in the cognitive science of Eleanor Rosch, which sparked a radical new view of cognition towards the end of the 20th Century.

[130] Steven Pinker, *The Language Instinct* (London: Penguin, 1994).

before. For example, children growing up in anarchic pidgin linguistic environments build their own creoles, with a much more stringent structure than the pidgin itself had.

This realisation is nothing new. In fact, it's millennia old. The Pre-Socrates considered thought and human existence to be inextricably intertwined. As quoted earlier, Parmenides wrote that "Thinking and being are one and the same." This famous statement is perhaps the first recorded expression of man's essential status as dwelling in thought, carried forward into the Cogito of Descartes and beyond. However, the latter already injected an emphasis on the subjective element ("*I* think therefore *I* am"), which implies a human agency not found in the original Parmenides dictum. In fact, the focus on personal selfhood found in the Cogito is fundamentally metaphysical. For Descartes, the implication is that thinking is emanating from a subject, when it could just as well be happening *to* a subject. As Heidegger argues: "Thus the originality native to identity as thought by Parmenides became subservient to the metaphysical understanding of Being."[131] Parmenides' statement is more pure, and a starting point along the lines of "there is thinking" could have provided a less metaphysical cornerstone for Descartes' reassessment of Western philosophy[132].

As Heidegger implies, identity is more than just the thinking of a subject – it's the foundation of human existence. Identity is an ongoing, active process of identification, where words and objects *belong* together. By emphasising the verb in the latter phrase, Heidegger highlights the continual action involved in identity. Paradoxically, identification implicitly entails difference. In the formulation of identity as equality, the fact that one example is equal to another implies that in some ways it is different, but these differences are pushed into the background. Only the common characteristics are considered. Even Heidegger's reworking of identity cannot get around the inherent

---

[131] Martin Heidegger, *Identity and Difference* (Chicago and London: The University of Chicago Press, 1969), p8.
[132] Renee Descartes, *Meditations on First Philosophy* (Cambridge: Hackett, 1993).

iteration in language. Indeed, it's visible from merely writing down his A *is* A. The second A looks the same on the page as the first. But if it was exactly the same it would be the first A in every way. The two As would have to exist in the same location as well as just offering a similar appearance. An even more accurate formulation would therefore be "A *is*", which is what Heidegger is trying to get at by arguing that identity makes an object the same as itself. Indeed, mathematical propositions are usually shorthanded in this way, such that a mere letter – say P – stands for an assertion in its entirety. But everyday language, in its attempt to identify symbolically, inadvertently promotes a simulated conception of identity rather than identity itself. As a result, difference carries out identity, and what we say something is, it never really is entirely – we've just chosen to ignore the singular distinctions of the iteration to which we are referring.

> "Every word instantly becomes a concept precisely insofar as it is not supposed to serve as a reminder of the unique and entirely individual original experience to which it owes its origin; but rather, a word becomes a concept insofar as it simultaneously has to fit countless more or less similar cases – which means, purely and simply, cases which are never equal and thus altogether unequal. Every concept arises from the equation of unequal things." [133]

This difference inherent in identity underlies the numeric as well. Without it, everything would be singular, and there would be no number greater than one. Counting requires phenomena to be successive examples of the same concept, but at the same time subtly different and multiple. Even though pure mathematics is considered to be entirely divorced from the material, due to its basis in Platonic ideals, it still works from this basis of numbers built up as iterations of one, identical concept.

---

[133] Friedrich Nietzsche, *On Truth and Lies in a Nonmoral Sense* (unpublished, 1873), p4.

Identity is also the primary engine of capitalist society, as Jürgen Habermas has pointed out with reference to Theodor Adorno:

> "Adorno was convinced that the principle of identity attained universal dominance in the measure that bourgeois society was subjected to the organizing principle of exchange: 'In exchange [bourgeois society] finds its social model; through it non-identical individual natures and achievements become commensurable, identical. The exploitation of the principle (of exchange) relates the whole world to what is identical, toward a totality.'"[134]

In this respect, money is therefore the ultimate symbol that brings the disparate together. Two different objects priced the same are considered economically identical, and enough cash can make anything the same as anything else. So, far from being merely the currency of one political system amongst many, money is the natural economic side-effect of a human existence based on a principle of idealised identity.

At a more fundamental level, difference is inherent in the formulation of Being and beings, which Heidegger argues is part and parcel of the ontological and theological (or "onto-theo-logical") essence of Being[135]. Being, as the underlying logic of phenomena, is essentially one step removed from beings. And this works both ways – beings, as the expression of Being, are therefore also different from it. However, this difference cannot itself be formulated, as this would bring it back into the realm of Being. Human existence forms the link between Being and beings, and computers would have to do the same if they were to become humanly intelligent. This is the very essence of consciousness. As Heidegger argues, identity comes from the

---

[134] Jurgen Habermas, *German 20th Century Philosophy: The Frankfurt School,* ed Wolfgang Schirmacher (New York: Continuum, 2000), p196.
[135] Martin Heidegger, *Identity and Difference* (Chicago and London: The University of Chicago Press, 1969).

event of appropriation (Ereignis). However, the historical separation of Being and beings, and Being's connection with consciousness, leads to the assumption that consciousness can be separated from existence and objectified. This separated consciousness is what computers have been designed to replicate.

So the expectation that computers will one day think for themselves is part and parcel of the materialisation of man as the subject of existence. Yet thinking machines also hold a deeply felt fear for mankind, expressed in popular culture from the psychotic HAL in Kubrick's sci-fi cinema classic *2001* to the homicidal anthropomorphic robots of the *Terminator* movies and the vision of mankind used as fuel in *The Matrix*. There is clearly a sense of unleashing something inhuman by creating a machine out of the essence of human intelligence. But the faculties accentuated in these machines are human faculties, and these are man-made machines. By highlighting and foregrounding certain attributes, something is lost. In order to objectify the subject, the subject must be clearly defined as a set of attributes and algorithms. Yet this effort seems naturally at odds with what it is attempting to achieve – the preservation of the subject.

> "The self, hypostatised by certain psychological schools as the 'core' of our being, subjective identity, is always already distorted by self preservation which in its institutionalised form, according to Horkheimer and Adorno, as hardening and petrifaction of conditions and thus of subjects, does away with the very self it was supposed to preserve."[136]

Why should this be the case? Why does the attempt to define the self appear to destroy the self? In particular, what exactly is "lost

---

[136] *No right to be a self: counterthinking,* Martin Hielscher, in *German 20ᵗʰ Century Philosophy: The Frankfurt School,* ed Wolfgang Schirmacher (New York: Continuum, 2000), p20.

in translation"? It would seem that the metaphysical programme to define an absolutely idealised essence for subjectivity is diametrically opposed to what it is to be a living individual, which is essentially spatio-temporally situated. This has been recognised long before the advent of the modern computer. For example, in the 19th century:

> "Space and time are for Schopenhauer the 'principium individuationis', ie the principle by means of which an individual is recognised as an individual. Outside of space and time no individuals exist."[137]

Viewed historically, it is no accident that the word "subject" has two meanings. The subject is a Janus-faced conception. One is the self, the other similar in sense to "topic", with all its implications of *topos*, the ancient Greek for place. The two intermingle and influence each other, so that the self gains an impression that it is something of substance. As Descartes' Cogito implies, the subject is the most important category of metaphysics, the lynchpin of Being. In contrast, Schirmacher argues "By weaning ourselves from the idealistic and materialistic orders of Being and Time we abandon the human individual as the substance which became subject."[138] But a question still remains: once the human individual is no longer substance, what does it become? Many materialist artificial intelligence theorists[139] argue that there is no consciousness beyond the substance of the human brain, making the complete understanding of how the mind works a future possibility – indeed, an inevitability. However, the question persists whether the current philosophical underpinnings of science are adequate to make this possibility a reality. Materialist AI research merely throws away one half of the mind/body dichotomy as being total

---

[137] ____, p20.
[138] Wolfgang Schirmacher, "Eco-sophia: the artist of life", *Research in Philosophy and Technology 9: Ethics and Technology*, ed Carl Mitcham (JAI Press: Greenwhich/London 1989), p125-134.
[139] In particular, Daniel Dennett.

fiction, which would seem a somewhat irresponsible way to treat thousands of years of intellectual history.

Out of the body experience

The separation of human mind from human body has been a perennial problem in philosophy for centuries. Heidegger's *Being and time* attempted to resituate existence back into a spatial-temporal context via the concept of Dasein (which can be translated into English as "being-there", putting the place back into essence). Heidegger's notion of *thrownness* describes how human beings find themselves *thrown into* this spatio-temporal world. They are conscious of an existence they didn't choose to have in an environment where a host of possibilities exist. But there is no absolute guidance as to which option to take at any given moment. Death plays the role of the ultimate horizon of these possibilities, the final limitation to what each human existence can achieve. As Schirmacher argues:

> "Mortality is the essential wager for man. No institution, no tradition survives its defenders; they will all be mere data in an electronic archive in a few technical decades."[140]

Yet there is a sense that subjectivity comes from outside, beyond an individual's control – to echo Althusser, when a person is "hailed", they become a subject. This takes the internal experience of being and puts its origin "out there" as something potentially visible and quantifiable. A number of world religions offer reincarnation as an answer to the mortality of everyday existence, making the subject an indestructible essence passed down through the generations. Other religions make the subject into a soul, transferred to an immortal plane of existence at the time of death.

---

[140] Wolfgang Schirmacher, "From the phenomenon to the event of technology", *Philosophy and Technology*, ed F Rapp (Reidel: Dordrecht 1983), *Boston Studies in the Philosophy of Science 80*.

In contrast, the post-modern decentred subject is considered purely contingent on the situation with no central continuous element, other than the continuity of events themselves. The subject is therefore made up of a series of iterations, linked sequentially but without the necessity of core characteristics which endure for the whole lifespan. This conception of the subject is described most famously by Deleuze and Guattari[141]. A subject without a continuous core would be particularly difficult to quantify as information and then to transform into the set of behavioural rules required for a computer program. The behavioural rules would vary from context to context through time. This would also be a problem for technology aimed at "downloading" a human consciousness into an artificial computation device. However, as Slavoj Zizek claims in *The Ticklish Subject*, the postmodern definition of a decentred self is itself problematic. Comparing it to the Hegelian conception of concrete universality where "Substance is subject", Zizek argues that

> "There is a clear contrast between this [ie Hegel's] subjectivisation and today's proliferation of postmodern 'identity politics' whose goal is the exact opposite, that is, precisely the assertion of one's particular identity, of one's proper place within the social structure."[142]

This leads to a depoliticised notion of society, where difference is catered for. The subject has been reduced to a process of subjectivization, where any kind of self is valid and all possibilities are allowed. Recent philosophical developments of Hegel's concrete universal, perhaps best exemplified by Alain Badiou's concept of Truth, point the way towards a historically contingent universal embodied in subjectivity. Art, as one of Badiou's Generic Truths, is set up in the subject. This ties in with Kant's transcendental imagination, an ancient concept

---

[141] Gille Deleuze and Felix Guattari, *Anti-Oedipus* (New York: Continuum, 2004).
[142] Slavoj Zizek, *The Ticklish Subject* (London: Verso, 1999), p208.

which harks back to the ideal visions of the pre-Socratic Anaximander and Plotinus[143]. However, it is hard to see how these transcendental experiences can lead anywhere but back to the age-old metaphysical distinction between mind and body.

In artificial intelligence research, the biggest problem posed by subjectivity is that of subjective experience itself, or 'Qualia'[144]. An individual's emotions and feelings about the world are fundamentally personal, although they can be communicated, and their physiological expressions recorded. Because of the latter, some theorists have tried to avoid the problem by merely analysing behaviour, whilst others have denied the importance of Qualia altogether[145]. "Every subjective phenomenon is essentially connected with a single point of view, and it seems inevitable that an objective, physical theory will abandon that point of view."[146] But this is essentially trying to model consciousness without its most important feature – conscious experience itself. The problem is, conscious experience is very much a singular thing. Other artificial intelligence theorists have taken on board the existence of Qualia, but tried to explain it in purely materialistic terms by the structure of the brain. Jeff Hawkins, for example, argues that "although hearing, touch, and vision work under similar principles in the neocortex, they are handled differently below the cortex."[147] In other words, although the brain sees generic patterns from all the senses at one level, each sense is wired up slightly differently before it reaches consciousness, and that wiring is also slightly different for each individual human. Although this would explain the varying feelings possible from a given phenomenon, it doesn't

---

[143] Anaximander argued that the first principle of all things was the Apeiron, limitlessness or indeterminacy, which was beyond all distinctions in being.
Plotinus divided the soul into two parts – an upper and lower part. The upper part or One was unchangeable and divine, whilst the lower one was the seat of personality, passions and vices. Like the Apeiron, the One transcended human existence.

[144] See John R Searle, *The Mystery of Consciousness* (London: Granta Books, 1997).

[145] Again, in particular, Daniel Dennett.

[146] Thomas Nagel, *What is it like to be a bat?* (*The Philosophical Review* LXXXIII, 4 (October 1974): 435-50).

[147] Jeff Hawkins, *On Intelligence* (New York: Times Books, 2004), p198.

help us understand the human ability to act in contradiction to those feelings – we are not merely reacting to sensual stimuli. It also trivialises the importance of these differences in wiring. Would each artificially intelligent being need some form of random attribution of how its senses affect its conceptualisation of the world, in order to give it the Qualia experienced by human beings? This leads us right back to the same interplay of identity and difference we've discussed at length already, and again makes the artificial being a simulation of the human, without necessarily pinning down the essence of consciousness. After all, the slightly different wiring in each individual human brain could be the result of some other process – it could be a symptom of consciousness rather than its direct cause. Qualia could be the by-product of how the choices each individual makes about life have trained his or her perceptions of the world. Indeed, our interpretations of phenomena are shaped by the preconceptions about the world we have built up over our lives.

Deleuze argues in *The Fold* and elsewhere that the subject is a point of view made up from its choices. Many choices are possible, but the worlds brought into being by each one cannot coexist. He coins the word *incompossible* from Leibniz to describe how we can imagine many worlds but only live in one. This has much in common with Nancy's singular plural in art discussed in the second chapter above, where the self is an entity continually folding the many possible perspectives into a singular personal perspective. At our core as human subjects lies a process of decision-making, the *genius decision* described by Klaus Ottman in his dissertation of the same name[148]. The artistic decision strives to present the non-presentable but is always doomed to failure. This is the true a priori of the subject, whence all our morality and universals stem – including science and technology. So could human decision be harnessed artificially to create a machine which can make choices, or would this be a paradox, the endeavour becoming a constant process of a dog chasing its tail? There are no conclusive theories yet about how Qualia come about, although we have

---

[148] Klaus Ottman, *The Genius Decision: The Extraordinary and the Postmodern Condition* (PhD dissertation, European Graduate School, 2002).

described one suggestion above from neuroscience. Consciousness is seen by many artificial intelligence theorists to be a side effect of powerful computational ability, particularly the massively parallel computing of the human brain. So a sufficiently powerful artificial computational device would simply gain consciousness as a byproduct of its sheer calculation ability. But this is a thinly disguised cop-out, offering no real analytical understanding of how the singular perspective of consciousness comes about in human existence. We will be returning to a few of the more promising theories, such as Hawkins's, in the final chapter, and putting forward a few speculations of our own.

Perceptions of self in the Internet age

On a more practical level, our everyday encounters with computing devices are changing the way we perceive ourselves. Sherry Turkle, in *Life on the Screen,* argues that the virtual self experienced over the Internet offers a new perspective on our concepts of personality. Certainly, the fluidity allowed by Internet communications means we can reshape how others view us much more according to our own imaginations – assuming those on the receiving end imagine things the same way. But the bigger question remains whether this really is a new mode of subjectivity, or just another way of showing how personal identity is already just another "life technique", as Wolfgang Schirmacher would describe it. Virtual identity is just one more tool in the arsenal of contextual identities we can use to keep on living. We are constantly recreating ourselves by our actions, with or without computerised communications. Heidegger argues that

> "the Order of Being is never simply given, but is itself grounded in some preceding act. *There is no Order of Being as a positive ontologically consistent Whole:* the false semblance of such an Order relies on the self-obliteration of the Act. In other words, the gap

of the Act is not introduced into the Order of
Being afterwards: it is there all the time as the
condition that actually *sustains* every Order of
Being."[149]

Heidegger also states, in The Word of Nietzsche, that for the
later Nietzsche "the 'will to power' stands before the mind's eye
as the fundamental characteristic of whatever is in being,". This
makes justice an attempt "to preserve Something that is *more*
than this or that particular person." [150] For Nietzsche, the Will to
Power is the primary revaluing/valuing force, placing value in
some essential way prior to truth. In other words, behind a drive
for truth lies a drive for power, embodied in the Act described by
Heidegger above. Does this mean that all value is relative? From
one perspective, yes – but relative values are always spatio-
temporally situated, so (as Heidegger often implies) must always
be considered historically in relation to a given group of people,
such as the art preservers we discussed in Chapter 2. "In the
work, truth is thrown toward the coming preservers, that is
toward a historical group of human beings."[151] Culture and
society ground values, giving them their sense of the absolute,
but this has no relevance without reference to that culture and
society.

However, despite arguing that the new virtual self created on the
Internet gives us an opportunity for greater self-recreation,
Sherry Turkle questions whether this really changes the self of
real life (or "RL", as the computer cognoscenti like to call it). In
Life on the screen, Turkle gives examples of how people can't
believe in their virtual selves. Virtual being may not help the
development of your real persona(s). Some may project their
virtual lives onto the real world – such as the online gamer in

---

[149] Martin Heidegger, *Identity and Difference* (Chicago and London: The
University of Chicago Press, 1969), p238
[150] Martin Heidegger, *The Question Concerning Technology* (New York: Harper
Torchbooks, 1977), p91
[151] *The origin of the work of art* in Martin Heidegger, *Basic Writings* (London:
Routledge, 1993), p200.

China who killed his friend over a magical item[152]. But in general research has shown no direct causal link between Internet behaviour and personality in "RL". This would seem to bear out Deleuze and Guattari's theory of the dividual self, with different characteristics developed for different contexts. The shy computer science expert in "RL" may become the heroic knight in an Internet role-playing game, but they will usually remain shy outside the virtual world. In other words, computer communications aren't so much a different medium for expressing the self, but a way of expressing a different self. The new context allows new forms of existence, but that context is required for these forms – they can't easily be transferred out of context.

One of the major long-term attractions of creating a computerised self is the potential to cheat death, although this could be argued is the motivation behind all "Great Works". Whereas the human body eventually breaks down in a way which can't be fixed, computers can supposedly be mended and upgraded. Evangelists of the digital age such as Ray Kurzweil and Hans Moravec look towards a future where the human body can be upgraded with cybernetic robotic parts, extending and enhancing its abilities. Eventually, the entire "wetware" of the body would be replaced with better artificial alternatives. Barring accidents, this could eventually extend life to an unlimited duration. The effect on human values would be unimaginable, as it would potentially remove mortality as the horizon of life. Existence gets its meaning from its finitude, and as a result many of our religious and cultural values get their importance from how they help us cope with death itself. This is already visible in the cultural changes of the last few centuries, as life expectancy has essentially doubled. Leisure has grown in importance, whereas mere survival was the primary concern just a few hundred years ago. But even when the average person could only expect to live into their thirties, a few lived to 60, 70 or more. It's hard to tell what cultural changes will occur when some can expect to live to 200, 300, or even more – ages which

---

[152] In 2005, Qiu Chengwei stabbed Zhu Caoyuan in the chest when he found out he had sold his virtual sword from the game Legend of Mir 3 for 7,200 Yuan.

nobody has yet experienced. What is likely is that the focus will shift away from childbirth as the creator of new life, towards artificial means of extending lives which already exist. In essence, the preservation of the metaphysical self would become the new goal. As Heidegger argues, "The uprising of man into subjectivity transforms that which is into object."[153] According to Heidegger, "Metaphysics is an epoch of the history of Being itself."[154] With human life made eternal by artificial means, the age of metaphysics would prevail as the final epoch, and the value ascribed to each specific individual increases.

The subjective focus of life-extending technologies is mirrored in art as well. As Jean-Luc Nancy argues, "the subject matter in painting is nothing other than subjectivity itself, which 'is the spiritual light lit up from within itself'"[155] Still, this is not so much a subject imposing ideals on the world, as an artist finding their subjectivity via their interaction with the world. "Modern subjectivism, to be sure immediately misinterprets creation, taking it as the sovereign subject's performance of genius."[156] Lyotard has underlined this with his example of the work of abstract artist Barnett Newman:

> "For Newman, creation is not an act performed by someone; it is what happens (this) in the midst of the indeterminate. If, then, there is any 'subject-matter', it is immediacy. It happens here and now. What [*quid*] happens comes later. The beginning is *that* there is... [*quod*]; the world, *what* there is."[157]

At least, with life-extending technologies, artificiality can be seen as an augmentation of man, rather than a simulated

---

[153] Martin Heidegger, *The Question Concerning Technology* (New York: Harper Torchbooks, 1977), p107.
[154] ____, p110.
[155] Jean-Luc Nancy, *The Muses* (Stanford: Stanford University Press, 1996), p53
[156] *The origin of the work of art* in Martin Heidegger, *Basic Writings* (London: Routledge, 1993), p200.
[157] Jean-Francios Lyotard, *The Inhuman* (Stanford: Stanford University Press, 1991), p82

replacement. Even with the human lifespan extended to a thousand years, whatever is at the core of consciousness could still remain, modified but not entirely replaced. Indeed, it could be argued that the entirety of mankind's technological existence has already taken considerable steps in this direction. In particular, Wolfgang Schirmacher's concepts of artificial life and "homo generator" define a technological existence focused on the continuation of life, rather than its replacement by machines.

Putting myself in the picture

It is hard to see why there is so much resistance to theories which infer an amount of subjective relativity in social matters. After all, many recent scientific theories also make the position of the observer paramount. General relativity makes no sense at all unless observers are placed in space and time. It is not the observer who is constant and objective, but the speed of light. What the observer experiences, and even their mass, is a function of their speed relative to what they are observing. For example, two objects travelling towards each other at the speed of light would appear to each-other to be aging twice as fast as they are from their own perspectives. Alternatively, two objects moving away from each other at the speed of light would appear to each-other to be suspended in time. Although these examples are clearly hypothetical, as travel at the speed of light is currently considered impossible, more muted versions of this phenomenon have already been used to estimate the age of the universe.

Similarly, Heisenberg's uncertainty principle[158] argues that you can't know a subatomic particle's speed and position at the same time. So the more precisely you observe one the less you will know about the other. Even more tellingly, observation of quantum particles actually dictates their state by the level of its precision, before which this state cannot be known. The path of a particle or orbit of an electron have no relevance in nature unless

---

[158] David Cassidy, "Heisenberg, Uncertainty and the Quantum Revolution", *Scientific American, 266* (May 1992), p106-112.

observed, and can't be predicted in advance. Similarly, predictions made from these observations can only give a statistical probability of future behaviour, not absolute certainty. The observer takes a necessarily active part in the physical state of the world, and can never be seen as objective and detached in the way normally conceptualised in traditional Newtonian science. How this active observation takes place remains a matter of extremely complicated quantum mechanics maths formulas, but as will be argued in the final chapter, certain characteristics of this process could help unravel some aspects of how human consciousness behaves the way it does.

It would show a distinct lack of understanding of science to simply translate the specific and very narrow observer-relativity phenomena described by physics to the social realm.[159] But it is a perennial problem of social science that it is nearly impossible to observe phenomena from an impartial viewpoint, in the way you can with bacteria in a Petri dish or apples falling from trees. The bias of the observer always gets in the way. To gain true understanding, areas of social science such as ethnography have gone in completely the opposite direction to objective distance, making participation a key element of the scientific process. Only by direct involvement can the truth be discovered, a process which Lacoue-Labarth calls "fictioning", explaining that this "signifies *transcendental installation*, the production (*Herstellung*) and erection (*Aufstellung*) of the stable (of the Same), without which nothing can be grasped or thought."[160] He even goes so far to posit fictioning as the essence of reason, stating that "Heidegger explains it in terms... of reason or transcendental imagination (*Einbildungskraft*)." This viewpoint would be an easy target for the opponents of idealism, except

---

[159] This is the kind of pseudo-scientific strategy in post-modernist philosophy which Alan Sokal and Jean Bricmont particularly criticised with their book *Intellectual Impostures* (London: Profile Books, 1998). They gave a number of examples of how scientific theories had been taken out of context and used in theoretical works of philosophy, in an attempt to make these theories seem more scientific.

[160] Philippe Lacoue-Labarthe, *Typography* (Stanford: Stanford Univserity Press, 1989), p71

that the idea of knowledge as a temporary human construct is borne out by quantum-era physics, particularly Heisenberg.

The empty subject – just a point of interest?

Taking all these arguments into account, we are left with a fairly vacant definition of subjectivity: namely, momentary points of active observation, connected only by an incomplete memory process. As the nexus of sensual perception, the self as singular point of view becomes a dot which can be transformed through history, but cannot be in two places at once by definition. Each self finds itself on its own "mission incompossible". This leads us to the major questions of the next chapter – how successful have attempts to make artificial intelligence using computer technology been so far, and is this because of a misconception of subjectivity? If the self is a singularity, the moral controversies over matter transportation or downloading brains into computers[161] are completely misplaced. Even if either one of these technologies do become possible, they would create two beings from one, not some paradoxical doppelganger of the same being. Both would have identical pasts, but the instant they became two separate entities they would bifurcate into two separate beings, and their selves would diverge. As we argued earlier in this chapter, a much more realistic alternative to completely artificial intelligence is a slow upgrade which leaves the human point of observation intact from enhancement to enhancement, rather than replacing it entirely. Wolfgang Schirmacher argues:

> "Human identity in opposition to machines
> proves to be abstract. This does not mean that
> man is a machine and should therefore be
> perceived one-sidedly, from a biologically

---

[161] For example, in Ray Kurzweil's *The Age of Spiritual Machines* (London: Texere, 2001). The controversy comes from the fact that both technologies are hypothesized as leaving behind the original from which the transportation is copied, or the brain downloaded. So two copies of the same person will exist. Should the old version be destroyed?

> behaviouristic viewpoint. Through machines
> certain human attributes are fulfilled – those
> attributes of which man is so painfully
> conscious, due to their absence, but which are
> so essential to his wholeness. In this sense the
> machine is human. It does not replace man; it
> compensates for his errors. It expands him in
> his potential..."[162]

In the essay "Can thought go on without a body?"[163], Lyotard
adds that the main job lying behind technical and scientific
research is to make thinking materially possible after the
destruction of the sun – which would take with it the grounding
earth described by Heidegger[164]. As we discussed earlier, this is
already the programme set out for artificial intelligence and
robotics research, which is attempting to extend our life spans by
upgrading our bodies piece by piece, until nothing of the
"original substrate" remains. Once mankind has transcended the
death of the physical body, next will come the death of the
planet (perhaps by mankind's own hand), the extinguishing of
the sun, the galaxy, the universe...

This progression would imply a humanity distinctly at odds with
its environment. The metaphysical view of subjectivity creates
this situation, as it places consciousness out of the body, rather
than inextricably linked to corporeal existence. Instead of this
theoretical subjectivity in opposition to the everyday practices of
the environment, Wolfgang Schirmacher has suggested an
intuition which he calls "eco-sophia", which is "wisdom, not
knowledge, and as concrete intuition it precedes the division of

---

[162] Wolfgang Schirmacher, "From the phenomenon to the event of technology",
Philosophy and Technology, ed F Rapp (Reidel: Dordrecht 1983), *Boston Studies
in the Philosophy of Science 80*.
[163] Jean-Francios Lyotard, *The Inhuman* (Stanford: Stanford University Press,
1991).
[164] Martin Heidegger, *Poetry, Language, Thought* (London: Harper Perennial,
1976).

theory and practice."[165] This intuition is not an ideal vision of transcendence, but a raw moment of appropriation at the point where the subject encounters the world. As Schirmacher argues, "Intuitive knowledge is neither an esoteric doctrine nor an irrelevant exploration of divine knowledge." [166] This works at the emotional level of compassion – similar to Heidegger's conception of "care"[167]. A physical reaction to the world acts as guide for cognitive response. Again, Schirmacher argues that:

> "Intuitive knowing, as it has been embodied in compassion, accompanies our life technology but does not reason over it. Discursive thinking, the reflective power of judgement, calculating science – they must all be transformed into basic technologies which contribute unnoticeably to continual self-perfecting below the threshold of our attention (and therefore of our egoistical intervention)."[168]

However, this compassionate, caring intuition still acts at the mental level, for the brain is just another physical organ. In fact, it would be wrong to discount the inextricable link between our imaginations and the physical. This is particularly obvious in our encounters with Internet communications, where pure text can evoke strong emotional reactions – even eroticism – in situations where direct physical encounter might not. Schirmacher argues that "It seems not everyone has heard that sex is a product of our imagination, its biological expression becomes stimulating only through artful application."[169] This should not be a surprise even for those who don't indulge in online fetish behaviour or

---

[165] Wolfgang Schirmacher, "Eco-sophia: the artist of life", *Research in Philosophy and Technology 9: Ethics and Technology*, ed Carl Mitcham (JAI Press: Greenwhich/London 1989), p125-134.

[166] Wolfgang Schirmacher, "The faces of compassion: Toward a post-metaphysical ethics", *ANALECTA HUSSERLIANA XXII*, 1987.

[167] Martin Heidegger, *Being and Time* (Oxford: Basil Blackwell, 1962).

[168] Wolfgang Schirmacher, "The faces of compassion: Toward a post-metaphysical ethics", *ANALECTA HUSSERLIANA XXII*, 1987.

[169] Wolfgang Schirmacher, "Net culture", *Poiesis 3*, (Toronto: EGS Press, 2001).

cybersex, as even traditional reproductive encounters require some form of fantasy or romance for stimulation. This kind of imagination still has its origins in instinct, although the encounter is steeped in artifice.

Schirmacher argues that intuition-driven knowledge is a combination of imagination with the world:

> "Determined by a self-generating activity we have to reformulate what it means to be human: mortality as well as natality are called into question again. [] Homo generator favours eternal revisions and safeguards the freedom of creation. What we clone is exactly this attitude of open generating and never a mere copy of anything (we leave that to primitive machines). Therefore, a biological copy of Mozart will never re-create the composer, and the media clone... has as many faces as people who feel themselves cloned by it." [170]

This is a key difference between pure mechanical reproduction and a human interpretation of phenomena. Although the digital era appears to have as one of its themes the ubiquitous exact copy, the homogenisation of culture in this media-dominated age isn't such a totalitarianism of the same. In fact, it could be a celebration of difference, because "...media clones humanity on a daily basis. Talk shows and chat rooms provide a media group therapy which lets even the weirdest people feel like everyone else."[171] In this sense, the message of media is now the primacy of choice as the goal of human existence. Digital media, particularly the Internet, eschew the few-to-many structure of the broadcasting age in favour of many-to-many. At the time of writing, the implications of this shift are still only starting to make themselves felt as social networking proliferates. But

---

[170] Wolfgang Schirmacher, *Cloning Humans with Media: Impermanence and Imperceptible Perfection*, http://www.egs.edu/faculty/schirmacher/schirmacher-cloning-humans-with-media.html (2000).
[171] Ibid.

today's media clones are no longer the identikit products of 20th century broadcast mass media, at least at the level of lifestyle. They now become members of virtual online communities of interest and participate more directly in the creation of their own mass culture.

Language categories – in the world or in humans?

So far, we have argued that the subject has gone through a multitude of guises, and has now been reduced to the focal point of consciousness as identity evolves through life. So objectifying the self is a fundamentally flawed proposition. Indeed, Nagel argues: "...if the facts of experience – facts about what it is like for the experiencing organism – are accessible only from one point of view, then it is a mystery how the true character of experiences could be revealed in the physical operation of that organism." [172] Cognitive science has also been moving away from a classical objectivist view, which holds that categorisation is inherent in the world and object characteristics are independent of human observers. The main empirical opposition to this classical view has come from prototype theory, primarily developed by Eleanor Rosch. Her work has been backed up experimentally by Berlin and Kay's research on colour categorisation, amongst others. Eleanor Rosch's prototype effects summarise Berlin and Kay by theorising an alternative to classic category theory, whereby all members of a set share a group of characteristics, without each member necessarily being required to have the same core list of characteristics. However, using examples from Berlin and Kay amongst others, Rosch showed that a category contains some members which are more characteristic than others, implying that not all members of a category are equal. She also showed that, at what is called the basic level, categories are rooted in the biology of human perception. Morphological properties and the bias of human senses tend to make these basic-level categories relatively universal across cultures. For example, the similarity of shape

---

[172] Thomas Nagel, *What is it like to be a bat?* (*The Philosophical Review* LXXXIII, 4 (October 1974): 435-50)

between objects appears to be what is initially used to group them together. With colour perception, the arrangement of receptors in the eye tends to push perception towards what are called focal colours – light and dark, red, yellow, blue, green, brown, purple, pink, orange and grey. Anthropological research has shown the ability to discern these focal colours even in cultures with very minimal colour terminology, and no specific terms for most of them. However, the focal colours merely predict the possible basic categories in a culture's colour terminology – they don't dictate the exact structure of these categories in a given language, nor how elaborate the categorisation will be. All languages at least have terminology for "warm" and "cool" colours, with the same focal colours included within each term. As the number of colour terms increases, a set pattern is followed – a language with three colour terms will have a separate category focused around red, for example. But the precise system of colour terminology depends on historical choices. It's also worth noting that in very basic systems, where more than one focal colour falls within a category, the focal colour chosen as prototypical by different test subjects varies, and could be ascribed to differing environmental experiences.

Rosch's findings have two implications. First, linguistic categories are primarily formed around concrete human experience, making it impossible to separate the categories of thought from physical perception. This backs up Schirmacher's claim that "Self and world cannot be played against one another, they belong together, inseparably, as reciprocal perceptive action." [173] However, the second implication is that whilst basic categorisation does follow some set patterns associated with human physical characteristics, the actual linguistic terminology found in a given culture is far from biologically determined. And beyond the basic level, categories are very much a product of culture and history. The variations between languages follow some patterns, but the specifics of each one are much more

---

[173] Wolfgang Schirmacher, *Cloning Humans with Media: Impermanence and Imperceptible Perfection*, http://www.egs.edu/faculty/schirmacher/schirmacher-cloning-humans-with-media.html (2000).

arbitrary. This yet again poses real problems for artificial intelligence systems. Artificial perception could be deliberately tuned in line with the biological biases already outlined for colour perception. But the wide variety of categorisation systems above the basic level backs up the argument that individual cultural perspective is paramount. Language systems are formed by a historical series of choices, which are only partly derived from permanent characteristics of the world. So an intelligent system using terms based purely on the latter fails to take sufficient account of the fact that humans are historically situated beings.

Categorisation systems come from analog memories rather than experience broken up and stored as discrete abstract characteristics dictated by the world on its own. This makes computer systems using such an abstract method for recognising input seriously flawed. As the current limited status of pattern recognition technology shows, matching characteristics in this way can never hope to replicate the human faculty in its entirety. Rosch's prototype theory outlines a cognition which operates at the basic level through aesthetic sense, rather than purely mental faculties. Recent neurological theory also claims that the same neurons participate in perception and action – so aesthesis and praxis really are inextricably intertwined in human physiology.[174] This aesthetic basis of thinking has wide-reaching implications. For example, Schirmacher points out that there are deeply ethical ramifications:

> "Three essential elements characterise an ethics unfolding from aesthetics within the horizon of post-nihilism: the surprising return of the monad, an aesthetic (not a cognitive) consciousness, and an expansion of our perceptive capacities once thought impossible

---

[174] Research cited in Jeff Hawkins, *On Intelligence* (New York: Times Books, 2004).

and which suggests a new quality of 'hyperperception'." [175]

We will be addressing the last of Schirmacher's points when we discuss the AI research of Jeff Hawkins in the next two chapters. For our argument so far, it is sufficient to say that, as Marshall McLuhan predicted, the global village has extended our vision far beyond the natural range of our senses. Greater neurological understanding could well enable perception devices which give us access to entirely new senses, rather than today's devices which merely convert sensory input to a form our existing senses can already perceive.

Rosch's prototype theory has radical implications for contemporary philosophy as well. Although it refutes the classical view that a core list of abstract characteristics define the members of a set, it also goes against many of the post-Wittgenstein philosophical theories we have quoted earlier. For example, Slavoj Zizek argues that

> "...the Universal genus is always one of its own species: there is universality only in so far as there is a gap, a hole, in the midst of the particular content of the universality in question, that is, in so far as, among the species of a genus, there is always one species missing: namely, the species that would adequately embody the genus itself." [176]

But according to prototype theory, there usually is a species which embodies the genus. On the other hand, this species does not consist of a precisely defined abstract set of characteristics, and is instead derived from concrete experience. It also sometimes varies from person to person within a culture, and even more from nation to nation. So the vagaries of differing

---

[175] Wolfgang Schirmacher, *Cloning Humans with Media: Impermanence and Imperceptible Perfection*, http://www.egs.edu/faculty/schirmacher/schirmacher-cloning-humans-with-media.html (2000).
[176] Slavoj Zizek, *The Ticklish Subject* (London: Verso, 1999), p103.

individual perception prevent a single fixed species epitomising a genus across all human culture. As we argued in previous sections of this chapter, our individual points of view give everyone a subtly unique perspective, even if there is a large proportion of common ground. Likewise, from Rosch's research into colour categories, the focal colour which epitomises a category does vary between various possible choices. But the essentially unattainable quality of the Ideal which we described earlier doesn't necessarily have to be ousted by this new cognitive theory. After all, the prototype is a concrete experience held in memory. Even if this prototype is made up of a host of different experiences of the same object, new encounters with that object won't precisely match the memory, and could augment it. The remembered prototype will still seem different from the example experienced in the world. So the sense that Being and beings only come together via human agency remains. As Schirmacher argues, "all perception is as active as it is experiential and brings forth an anthropomorphic world."[177] If, as Rosch argues, our cognitive categories are at the basic level dependent on our bodies, we cannot escape from seeing the world in human terms. With different (or no) bodies we would see the world in an alternative way.

Rosch's prototype theory would appear to leave artificial intelligence high and dry in its effort to mimic human thinking. With cognition so inextricably intertwined with our individual physical experiences of the world, it would appear to be impossible to recreate it artificially using abstract algorithms. Lengthy study of how humans form categories would be required, which may never result in a generalised, universal system. The process could be entirely contingent, with different methods necessary for different types of category. Indeed, this would already appear to be the case, as George Lakoff's wide-ranging study in *Women, Fire, and Dangerous Objects* shows. Citing anthropological research, Lakoff defines a number of criteria for membership in cognitive categories across world

---

[177] Wolfgang Schirmacher, *Cloning Humans with Media: Impermanence and Imperceptible Perfection*, http://www.egs.edu/faculty/schirmacher/schirmacher-cloning-humans-with-media.html (2000).

cultures, including metonymy and metaphor. Yet again, it would appear that the criteria for a subset of human thought – in particular mathematics and the "hard" sciences such as physics – has been applied to all human thought, and then used as a basis for a generalised intelligence. The end result has been so-called thinking machines which really only represent a small subset of human thought processes. The full gamut of the mental faculty is much larger. The experiential nature of categories means that they are never fixed, instead changing with further experience – the infamous Black Swan scenario. As Hielscher puts it, "To experience means not to return the same as one was before and no longer to know what had previously rendered the world plausible. Experience takes one beyond appropriation and brings one to an other."[178] New experiences have the ability to radically alter our view of the world, and any system based on a fixed set of characteristics fails to address this. Habermas describes an interplay of the subject and the world where the subject changes in order to improve its control over the world, stating that "The I acquires its inner organisational form in the measure that, in order to coerce external nature, it coerces the amorphous element in itself, its inner nature." [179]

The experiential nature of categories has even deeper implications for the objective view of the world itself. If our language categories are not fixed, but vary between individuals and over time, objectivity itself is rendered fluid. This has led Deleuze to coin a new term to replace the object – the objectile[180], a similar idea to the term "eventity" which we coined in a previous chapter of this book. The object can no longer be viewed as a static entity but must be seen as situated in time, since it changes its nature with time. Similarly, the subject becomes a "superject"[181], a term coined by Whitehead. The

[178] Martin Hielscher, *No right to be a self* in *German 20th Century Philosophy: The Frankfurt School,* ed Wolfgang Schirmacher (New York: Continuum, 2000), p32.
[179] Jürgen Habermas in *German 20th Century Philosophy: The Frankfurt School,* ed Wolfgang Schirmacher (New York: Continuum, 2000), p188
[180] Gille Deleuze, *The Fold* (Minneapolis: University of Minnesota Press, 1993), p19.
[181] ____, p20.

superject is in a constant state of transcendental flux, just as objects have a historical trajectory.

Going places, or superjects in motion

The traditional argument against relativism is that it offers no basis for morality. If all viewpoints are equal on some level, then there is no way of determining good from evil. Certainly, a purely relativist stance does undermine absolute moral values – and with them absolutist views of the individual. However, the nomadic view of the subject we have outlined above doesn't make it something which is in such a constant state of change as to never have moments of rest. Deleuze argues that, "Such is the basis of perspectivism, which does not mean a dependence in respect to a pregiven or defined subject; to the contrary, a subject will be what comes to the point of view, or rather what remains in the point of view."[182] This last idea of "what remains" is fundamental. What remains is memory, which is an imperfect record of historical points of view. While memory gives the subject continuity, the monadic dividual remains nomadic, as Deleuze and Guattari have asserted at length[183]. Despite the continual change inherent in the "body without organs", the one constant for the post-modern schizophrenic human is the activity of perception and cognition – the constant process of formulating a point of view. "Every point of view is a point of view on variation." So relativism, "is not a variation of truth according to the subject, but the condition in which the truth of a variation appears to the subject." [184]

This perspectivist view of the subject is not quite the same as classic relativism – if such a thing ever existed anyway. "Perspectivism is clearly a pluralism, but it thus implies by its name distance and not discontinuity (certainly no void is given

---

[182] ____, p19.
[183] Gille Deleuze and Felix Guattari, *A Thousand Plateaus* (New York: Continuum, 2004).
[184] Gilles Deleuze, *The Fold* (Minneapolis: University of Minnesota Press, 1993), p20.

between two points of view)."[185] The historical contextualisation of the subject works both ways. Whilst it denies absolutes outside history, conventional values within a historical period remain as quasi-absolutes. Yet again, this conceptualisation has been criticised as unable to distinguish between two contexts with differing viewpoints. However, Deleuze has pointed out that this aspect of perspectivism has long been realised as a problem. For example, he mentions in *The Fold* that:

> "...Leibniz constructs the 'table' of cases that refers to point of view as jurisprudence or the art of judgement. It comprises the need to find the correct point of view – or rather, the best – without which disorder or even chaos would reign."[186]

But how do you work out this "best point of view"? Therein lies the biggest question of all. A potential answer could be formulated from Heidegger's concept of Ereignis. Although perspectivism replaces Reality with a collection of individual realities, it doesn't deny the existence of a world outside the subject, just the impossibility of seeing that world without the spectacles of a point of view. Just as scientific theories are refuted or corroborated by repeatable evidence, so Ereignis reveals when points of view veer too far away from the truth. Deleuze argues that:

> "A soul always includes what it apprehends from *its* point of view, in other words, inflection. *Inflection is an ideal condition or a virtuality that currently exists only in the soul that envelops it.* Thus the soul is what has folds and is full of folds."[187]

But hiding within the folds is the potential for aletheia – the revealing/concealing of truth. Lying at the heart of every subject,

---

[185] _____, p20.
[186] _____, p21.
[187] _____, p22.

a moment of appropriation founds perspective, unifying the monad, if only for an instant. "The world of metaphysics is beyond, and closes repetition... the monad is this fixed point that infinite partition never attains, and that closes infinitely divided space." [188] In this respect, the "windowless monad" is not an entity with no outside links – it just has no direct outside links. In Deleuze's depiction, folded drapes escape the windowless upper room, although their relation to its interior remain obscure. Similarly, no direct link to the noumenal world of ideas is possible, but it can be alluded to.

In Leibniz's philosophy, windowless monads merely exist in pre-programmed harmony with each other. The individual subject is such a windowless monad – a singularity that defies repetition. It cannot be part of an iterated series. Its particular folding of the world tends towards the unique. This is the locus of where art and individuality coincide. But folding is the common ground which brings together Being and beings. "We go from inflection to inclusion just as we move from the event of the thing to the predicate of the notion, or from 'seeing' to 'reading'." [189] Recent discoveries in quantum mechanics show a remarkable parallel to the concept of windowless monads acting in harmony with each other, a subject we will be returning to in the final chapter of this book.

According to Deleuze, both Liebniz and Whitehead agree that the first component of the event is extension. "Extension exists when one element is stretched over the following ones, such that it is a whole and the following elements are its parts."[190] Deleuze explains how this process connects to the body and its senses, yet without a direct causal relationship between the individual perspective and its external influences:

> "Conscious perception has no object and does not even refer to a physical mechanism of excitation that could explain it from without: it

---

[188] ____, p28.
[189] ____, p41.
[190] ____, p77.

refers only to the exclusively physical mechanism of differential relations among unconscious perceptions that are comprising it within the monad."[191]

In this chapter, the concept of the subject has been traced through various historical threads of terminology, and some recent ideas about how we should re-conceive ourselves have been discussed. Along the way, we have moved far from the definitions of the subject with which we started. Instead of being defined in terms of external properties, the subject is characterised as an enclosed monad, forever obscured from view. Individuals can find ephemeral harmonies with temporal worldly phenomena. But without direct knowledge of the self, these harmonies cannot be predicted by studying the worldly phenomena nor attempting to build an idealised model of personality. No knowledge of the latter can ever be complete. In the next chapter, we will be discussing 20th century attempts to create artificial intelligence and recent theories about how close we will get in the 21st century. Using what has been discussed about art, computing and subjectivity, it will become apparent just how far we are from computers which can make art – but also where more fruitful alternatives might lie, and how digital technology can have a place in creative processes.

---

[191] ____, p93.

Chapter 5
Being artificial

If, as Lyotard argues in *The Inhuman*, science and technology are fundamentally endeavouring to free thought from material corporeality, this is surely most evident in computer technology, and particularly in research into artificial intelligence. The infamous Turing Test[192] has turned the quest for artificial intelligence into an exercise in Baudrillardian simulation – if it fools you into thinking it's human, it must be human. Joseph Weizenbaum's ELIZA psychoanalysis expert system of the 1960s managed to achieve this for some of its users. However, most of the theoretical research into computing in the 20th century has focused on modelling the human mind at a more essential level. The lack of understanding of the founding decision, or moment of truth, which sits at the centre of the human subject (or Dasein) and is particularly evidenced in the artistic process, would imply that computers are really just products of a science blinded by instrumental technology. The mind is treated as a computing instrument, rather than the judgement centre for the living human experience of truth. This drive to render ourselves obsolete with our own creations seems thoroughly questionable. Shouldn't computers be our slaves? So why do we want them to do the fun things in life, like art? Surely we should keep those for ourselves. This is the end result of a scientific, moralistic culture which has put the living human subject out of the picture, replacing it with a machinated image of the self, or a greedy materialistic conception of the self derived from capitalist (or Soviet Communist) economics.

One of the most famous refutations of the possibility of artificial intelligence is Hubert Dreyfus's *What computers can't do*[193], which was updated to *What computers **still** can't do* in 1979. Dreyfus takes a phenomenological approach to his critique of AI

---

[192] For a detailed critique of the Turing Test, see Mark Halpern, "The Trouble with The Turing Test", *The New Atlantis Journal of Technology & Society*, Number 11, Winter 2006, p42-63.
[193] This version was originally published in 1972.

technology, broadly similar in a number of its arguments to critiques we have adopted in this paper. Although a lot has happened in the computing world since his book was written, the mainstream of AI research is still following methods Dreyfus criticises, so his comments remain relevant. Indeed, they show how little has been learned in the intervening decades. In the most recent version of the book Dreyfus outlines a number of different strategies in AI research. The traditional method, at which the lion's share of the original treatise is aimed, is dubbed Good Old-Fashioned AI (GOFAI). But he also defines a few other subtypes, such as Symbolic AI. This attacks the AI problem from the computational point of view we have already defined in earlier chapters. With Symbolic AI, the world is broken into definable semantic representations and rules which can be programmed into a computer system. Whilst more complex processes like recursive algorithms (see above) can be applied to Symbolic AI, this still doesn't allow it to escape from the difficulty of defining the symbols and rules in the first place. We have already addressed the main problems with this information-based approach in Chapter 3.

However, at the same time as GOFAI has shown its fruitlessness, neural networks have taken up the challenge instead. The workings of neural networks have also been outlined in Chapter 3. Also known as Connectionist AI, this approach sidesteps the problems of Symbolic AI. Instead of requiring problems to be defined as symbols, Connectionist AI uses parallel systems which learn abstract patterns through a process of trial and error. As Dreyfus comments, "Neural networks do appear to have learning ability; but in situations of supervised learning, it is really the person who decides which cases are good examples who is furnishing the intelligence."[194] Once the network has been through its process of learning, it becomes static unless put through further teaching. This is clearly not the same as a human intelligence, which is in a constant state of development (and eventual degradation), even if the process slows down considerably in adulthood. The neural

---

[194] Hubert L. Dreyfus, *What computers still can't do* (Cambridge, Massachussetts: The MIT Press, 1992), pxxxix

net may be receiving reinforcement learning instead of supervised learning – that is, graded input from the environment rather than god-like teaching – but it still has no active ability to learn of its own accord by going beyond its preset parameters. This is a key part of what it means to be humanly intelligent.

Still, Symbolic AI continues to have its proponents, and one of the foremost amongst them is Douglas B Lenat. With his Cyc program, Lenat has tried to push Symbolic AI much further by using an ontological approach to define the rules of common sense. Despite grand claims of success, Lenat isn't really doing anything new, except in scale. Cyc's CycL language uses the recursive functions discussed in Chapter 3 to define its commonsense knowledge, but is still essentially subservient to human beings for inputting the individual snippets. Like the Connectionist AI approach, the system has no ability to generate its own knowledge – something which the most recent newborn child can do, as can a large proportion of the animal kingdom. Lenat's Cyc can be addressed by the same set of arguments Dreyfus applies to GOFAI.

Even the Connectionist AI neural network approach emphasises learning knowledge which is essentially given – where the weighing of alternatives is always evident. This strategy is still stuck in the world of ontology. It doesn't address how ontology and Being come into existence in the first place through Ereignis. A much more complex task would be to teach a machine to make decisions where the different choices available are identical according to ontology, or so dissimilar that there is no way to compare them. It is the ability to make these kinds of decisions which defines humanity. From the perspective of ontological reason, the most "difficult" decisions for humans appear random and arbitrary, but after the fact they can be fitted into a newly emergent schema. We all make such decisions – the great do so allegedly more adeptly and confidently than the masses, but everyone is born with the potential. Although this may sound like the age-old free will argument recast for a philosophical era after post-modernism, there are differences. This is not an entirely free choice – the options are still limited by the world. However, the process of choosing is not predetermined by an existing set of rules, as the worldly limitations are constantly in flux and unpredictable.

As we argued in the previous chapter, this kind of decision comes from an intuitive knowing which is more akin to compassion than speculative knowledge. Dreyfus explains that "According to Plato, cooks, for example, who proceed by taste and intuition, and poets who work from inspiration, have no knowledge: what they do does not involve understanding and cannot be understood."[195] Intuition has long been recognised as the basis of knowledge, the foundation upon which it is built. Aristotle points out in his Nicomachean Ethics that the interpretation of understanding always relies on intuition. But the focus has always been on the formalisation of knowledge after the intuitive process has completed. Leibniz tried to work out binary elements of a formal language for conceptualising objects. His algebra of the mind was intended to make all things calculable. George Boole tried to systematise that algebra with Boolean logic. Then Babbage envisaged his Analytic Engine and Turing talked of discrete state machines. As explained in Chapter 3, computers can relate anything to anything – but only if it can be represented symbolically (ie as information). "Even an analogue computer, provided that the relation of its input to its output can be described by a precise mathematical function, can be simulated on a digital machine."[196] For example, a number of classic analog musical synthesisers have been recreated on computer systems, and the results are generally regarded to be virtually indistinguishable from the original instruments.

However, although a current Von Neumann machine-based digital computer could be used to simulate analog processes, this doesn't address the core of the critique we are outlining. It is not the digitisation of information which is the problem. Even the conception of human pattern recognition as the central process in intelligence is too passive – we don't just recognise patterns that

---

[195] ____, p63
[196] ____, p63

are already there, but also bring some forth whilst leaving others unnoticed. In other words, we participate in them from our perspective as subjects. As Max Wertheimer argued in *Productive Thinking*, thought moves forward by the intuitive recognition of anomalies, which force reconsideration of previous systematic assumptions – a small-scale parallel to Kuhn's paradigm shifts[197]. Similar ideas have been applied to the neurology of perception by Jeff Hawkins, which we will be returning to later in this chapter. Dreyfus's emphasis on chess playing as an example of the weakness of Symbolic AI betrays the date when he was writing. The most recent intro, written in 1992, still predates the success of Deep Fritz, which in October 2002 drew 4-4 with chess champion Vladimir Kramnik, and Garry Kasparov was defeated by Deep Blue in 1997. Kramnik was Kasparov's successor as world chess champion. But these AI successes don't really diminish Dreyfus's overall argument, which is about wider issues than mastering games with clearly defined rules.

Dreyfus, like any good phenomenologist, is trying to put the human body back into the picture – to reinstate the wetware alongside the hardware, so to speak. The fundamental flaw in the notion of the computer as an intelligent entity is that the real thinking is done in the programming, not by computer (or user) at all. The failure therefore lies in the programmer's inability to foreground their own input into the systems. When an expert system such as ELIZA or Lenat's Cyc is programmed, logical connectives are created between all the disparate "knowledge statements". The implication involved in a logical connective makes one statement the logical consequence of another. This may be perfectly valid for mathematical statements, but for statements about the world it necessarily involves a reduction of truth. The decision over what to remove for this logical process work is performed by the programmer, not by the computer. Yet this "finding the same" between statements is the essence of human being through language. This is the discovery of

---

[197] Thomas Kuhn, *The Structure of Scientific Revolutions* (Chicago: University of Chicago Press, 1996).

repetitive iteration in the constant change that is "raw" existence, described in the previous chapter.

We have already criticised current AI research for its continuing attempt to fulfil the Turing test, and thereby simulate intelligence rather than actually recreate it. The question revolves around whether there's really a difference between the two; and if there is, whether that difference matters. Dreyfus details the assumptions underlying AI research, which he categorises as the biological, the psychological, the epistemological, and the ontological. Here, as with Dreyfus's use of chess computing as an example of AI failure, the argument is a little dated. With the biological assumption, the brain is assumed to be digital computer at the neuron level, when current research points towards it being more analogue and continuous in operation, despite neurons having essentially binary firing and non-firing states. However, certain research programmes such as the Redwood Neuroscience Institute are focusing their investigations on analysing the way the brain actually works as a basis for AI design.

The psychological assumption is that the mind is a device operating on bits of information according to formal rules, which is how we get to the notion that minds could be separated from bodies. Although this isn't quite metaphysics, it is a direct result of the historical mind/body dichotomy stemming from metaphysics. Allied to the psychological assumption is the epistemological one, that all knowledge can be expressed as logical, Boolean relations. Dreyfus argues "Does it justify the epistemological assumption that all non-arbitrary behaviour can be formalized?"[198]. Our answer would be that arbitrary behaviour cannot be discounted from intelligence, because intuitive action can appear arbitrary until the true depth of understanding behind it becomes clear. We have already addressed the overriding problems with the ontological assumption earlier in this chapter and the previous one. However, it's still necessary to explain why it has remained so

---

[198] Hubert L. Dreyfus, *What computers still can't do* (Cambridge, Massachussetts: The MIT Press, 1992), p195

key to AI research. As argued elsewhere, this is due to the many discoveries of the "hard" sciences in the 20th century. Dreyfus explains, "But if the ontological assumption does not square with our experience, why does it have such power? ... the myth is fostered by the success of modern physics."[199] But not every lesson from modern physics has been learned – in particular the shift away from the Newtonian paradigm. This has left AI research within the objectivist model, with its attendant metaphysical assumptions. Heidegger explains how the scientific approach precludes the possibility of discovering the truth about nature:

> "Scientific representation, for its part, can never decide whether nature, through its objectness, does not rather withdraw itself than bring to appearance the hidden fullness of its coming to presence. Science cannot even ask this question, for, as theory, it has already undertaken to deal with the area circumscribed by objectness."[200]

Chief amongst these ontological assumptions, however, is that you can separate thought from the body, as Dreyfus explains:

> "Looking back over the last ten years of AI research we might say that the basic point which has emerged is that *since intelligence must be situated it cannot be separated from the rest of human life.*"[201]

This fact has been greatly elaborated by George Lakoff[202]. Lakoff shows that, contrary to received wisdom, language doesn't necessarily embody the way we see the world, although

---

[199] ____, p212
[200] Martin Heidegger, *The Question Concerning Technology* (New York: Harper Torchbooks, 1977), p174.
[201] Hubert L. Dreyfus, *What computers still can't do* (Cambridge, Massachussetts: The MIT Press, 1992), p62.
[202] In particular, in George Lakoff, *Women, Fire, and Dangerous Things* (Chicago and London: The University of Chicago Press, 1987).

it does highlight certain aspects over others. Instead, language is founded on basic cognitive categories, for example the basic colours, which are effectively universal across the human race. Although subdivisions follow certain rules (eg the colour terminology research cited in *Women, Fire and Dangerous Objects*, and discussed in the previous chapter here), these are based on psychological and biological criteria – such as the way the human eye processes colour, or the differentiation in physical shape between animals experienced in the local environment. In other words, how the world is conceptualised doesn't just come from the world, but how the human body encounters that world. This could easily be replicated in an AI system, with enough understanding of human biology and how that affects perception. But it still wouldn't account for cultural and individual differences. Although the colour research cited by Lakoff shows how increasingly complex categorisation does follow basically the same patterns in every culture, it doesn't explain how a culture moves up the ladder of complexity in each individual culture. This is clearly a matter of historical context.

The necessity of situating intelligence within a human interacting with the world is not just at the level of higher order knowledge, but works at the very basic linguistic level of categorisation. As Lakoff argues in *Woman, Fire and Dangerous Objects*, even the basic categories are derived from concrete examples experienced in the world, and do not come from preordained, abstract and idealised criteria as the classical theory of categorisation would argue. These categories also incorporate the experience of how one would interact with them. For example, chairs involve the activity of sitting, which is clearly not a characteristic inherent in the object itself. This is only relevant to humans, and wouldn't be a factor for beings which don't sit down. In a sense, the instrumental Enframing of objects by technology is part and parcel of our categorisation of the world – just as Heidegger's discussions of the origins of techne show[203]. Rosch discusses two levels of category – basic and superordinate. From experimental work, Rosch discovered that

---

[203] See Chapter 2.

the characteristics of basic categories, such as "chair", are defined in terms of the characteristics of a prototype – eg a specific, commonly experienced chair for the individual in question in their cultural context. But despite being more abstract and general, superordinate categories such as "furniture" still refer to the characteristics of concrete examples. In both cases, although the concepts have been abstracted into a prototype, this is still wholly based on concrete experience, which will be different for every individual. Taking "chair" as our example again, the prototypical category will be basically the same within a culture because the most commonly encountered chair will form the prototype of that category, and will be essentially the same type of chair across that culture. But there will still be variations between individuals.

The major implication of this cognitive science for artificial intelligence is that AI cannot hope to mimic the human mind using the classical theory of categorisation, which states that every member of a category shares a fixed set of characteristics equally with all the others. We have already discussed in the previous chapter how Wittgenstein's theory of family resemblances has moved thought beyond this classical approach. Dreyfus's work, however, predates most of the recent research derived from Wittgenstein, and focuses on the physical context. Even then, just attempting to contextualise statements about the world in a Symbolic AI system isn't in itself sufficient, because it offers no method for controlling how far that context needs to extend. The AI system could end up requiring all world knowledge. As Dreyfus puts it,

> "On the one hand... there must always be a broader context; otherwise we have no way to distinguish relevant from irrelevant facts. On the other... there must be an ultimate context, which requires no interpretation; otherwise there will be an infinite regress of contexts. [] Instead of a hierarchy of contexts, the present

situation is recognised as a continuation or
modification of the previous one." [204]

Contextualising intelligence spatially is clearly just the
beginning. So much of our motivation comes from physical and
emotional needs that the calculations of mental ingenuity would
be rendered irrelevant if they didn't take them into account.
Dreyfus states that "our concrete bodily needs directly or
indirectly give us our sense of the task at hand, in terms of which
our experience is structured as significant or insignificant."[205]
Indeed, a major part of intelligence is involved in working out
exactly what the body wants, in order to satisfy its requirements,
because "human beings... in discovering what they need they
make more specific a general need which was there all along but
was not determinate." [206] This particularisation of desire again
emanates from the individual as a focal point of view, further
underlining our earlier arguments. "In such a creative discovery
the world reveals a new order of significance which is neither
simply discovered nor arbitrarily chosen." [207]

While it is far from a trivial realisation that computers would
need to have full human experience of life to act like full
humans, that is only part of the issue. It is still not at all clear
how humans *become* conscious – how Heidegger's concepts of
aletheia, Ereignis and truth fulfil themselves in human cognition,
or (in Kant's terms) how imagination meets the world in the
Idea, or (in Hegel's terms), how substance becomes subject.
However, it seems certain that this process is not purely
mechanical. There is something fundamentally incompatible
with the idea of free choice or the will, and anything
mechanistic. This is particularly true of our appreciation of
artistic form, as Lyotard illustrates: "When one judges a body to
be weighty, the opposite judgement is excluded. Form is not

[204] Hubert L. Dreyfus, *What computers still can't do* (Cambridge,
Massachussetts: The MIT Press, 1992), p222.
[205] ____, p276.
[206] ____, p277.
[207] ____, p277.

beautiful in the same way that a body is weighty." [208] In summation, today's so-called artificial intelligences are merely extensions of the intelligence of their creators – they have no real independent intelligence of their own. The will they exhibit is that of those who programmed them.

Recent AI research

John Searle argues that there are different levels of belief in the possibility of an artificially created intelligence, which he calls Strong and Weak AI.[209] Strong AI refers to the notion that the brain is just a computer, and creating a fast enough computer will create a brain because consciousness and Qualia are just a figment of our imaginations. Weak AI merely argues that computers are useful in doing simulations of brain functions. According to Strong AI, the mind is a program, and could run on any hardware. Searle refutes it with his now famous proof called The Chinese Room. This argues that understanding how to deal with a language syntactically does not mean you understand it semantically.[210] This is precisely what computers do. Referring to the teleological programme for humanity to survive the death of the Sun, Lyotard argues that "theoretically the solution is very simple: manufacture hardware capable of 'nurturing' software at least as complex (or replex) as the present-day human brain, but in non-terrestrial conditions."[211] But as we argued in the previous chapter, the question of intelligence isn't just one of mind software running on brain hardware – or an entirely artificial computer. For a start, there is the weakness of current

---

[208] Jean-Francois Lyotard, *Lessons on the Analytic of the Sublime* (Stanford: Stanford University Press, 1994), p205.
[209] John R Searle, *The Mystery of Consciousness* (London: Granta Books, 1997).
[210] The Chinese Room contains non-Chinese speakers, who are fed input commands in Chinese. They then consult a rulebook on how to deal with these symbols (which are incomprehensible to them), and feed the answers to the output, again in Chinese. These answers may be linguistically correct, but the room occupants have no idea of the meaning of the symbols they have been manipulating.
[211] Jean-Francois Lyotard, *The Inhuman* (Stanford: Stanford University Press, 1991), p14.

Von Neumann machine-based computers, which Lyotard sums up eloquently:

> "as Dreyfus argues, human thought doesn't think in a binary mode. It doesn't work with units of information (bits) but with intuitive, hypothetical configurations. It accesses imprecise, ambiguous data that don't seem to be selected according to pre-established codes or readability." [212]

Instead, it has been argued that human thought is a totalised process of pattern recognition. Jeff Hawkins reckons human memory stores patterns and that the nature of intelligence is based on our ability to match the phenomena we encounter to invariant forms held in our brains. He does at least explain that these forms are not lists of characteristics which must be checked off. So this would preclude the database approach used by traditional Von Neumann machine-based computer systems. However, his theory of invariant forms still seems somewhat old-fashioned, and doesn't explain the element of judgement in our recognition of similarity and difference. Although his hypothesis that the senses merely supply pattern data for a general-purpose mental process is insightful, it remains a static view of our conceptual faculties. For example, he argues that "A face is a face precisely because two eyes, a nose, and a mouth always appear together. The same can be said for chairs, cars, trees, parks and countries."[213] He offers no proof that there really is an invariant form held in the brain which remains constant, and can't explain our ability to recognise cases which don't have all the characteristics required. He merely describes how cases which don't immediately fit the pattern automatically trigger greater attention. But we would still recognise a face with just one eye in the middle as a face, even if such a cyclopean visage would generally be considered monstrous.

---

[212] ____, p15.
[213] Jeff Hawkins, *On Intelligence* (New York: Times Books, 2004), p126.

It would seem much more plausible that each invariant is actually augmented when a new physical example of the form in question is encountered in the world. Hawkins seems to imply that there's an abstract structure held in the brain, when in fact it could just as easily be a whole series of concrete examples from a specific individual's life experience which have been connected together. For example, our memories of all the dogs we have ever encountered are interconnected, so another animal with enough in common with these memories will also be called a dog. But these memories will also be connected to other categories – say hair, leads, ballgames, or any number of dog-related experiences. These will be subjective and vary unpredictably from person to person.

Again, what appears to be missing is how humans have to make a judgement between past and new experiences. Hawkins' theory would imply that the process is automatic based on pattern recognition from memory. While this would seem appropriate for non-controversial experiences, how we fit borderline cases into a category – or come up with a new one – remains a mystery. His theory also conveniently ignores the motivation which links our recognition of the world and our actions. Merely figuring out how our brains understand our experiences doesn't explain how we act upon that understanding. To be fair on Hawkins, he isn't trying to create artificial humans, and explicitly states that this is not his aim. He simply believes the core of human intelligence is the neocortex, and that understanding how this works will open the door to machines with much greater powers than current Von Neumann-based systems. But even though this kind of intelligence may be an important part of what separates mankind from other animals, on its own it's essentially purposeless. As Nietzsche remarked, "man would sooner have the void as his purpose than be devoid of purpose"[214]. Humans need motivation, and their ability to find it without logical rationale is fundamental to mankind's essence.

---

[214] Friedrich Nietzsche, *Beyond Good and Evil* (London: Penguin, 2003).

Lyotard also warns against the mechanisation of human judgement:

> "This picture inevitably recalls the description Kant gave of a thought process he called reflective judgement: a mode of thought not guided by rules for determining data, but showing itself as possibly capable of developing such rules afterwards on the basis of results obtained 'reflexively'." [215]

It would be hard to deny that humans think via analogy. Most new experiences are related by saying one thing is another different thing (the former is the figure, the latter the ground). So the characteristics of one are used to think about the other. These characteristics grow with the bodily perception of the ground. Language itself could be considered a giant analogy – the differences in oral or written code standing as analogies to the differences in the world, albeit highly abstract analogies. Structuralist theory argues essentially this, although structural linguistics relates the symbolic realm of language to our mental conception of the world, not the world itself. However, although analogy would seem like a logical process and therefore readily described as a computational algorithm, in reality the leap from figure to ground requires judgement and decision in the way we have already discussed. Statements of analogy and metaphor bring two disparate elements together in order to transfer characteristics from one to the other. This forcing of identity is synthetic – the figure and ground are clearly not the same, and the analogy is a creative act. To make the analogy – and to understand it – necessitates a mental conceit as the two disparate elements are forced together. "Real 'analogy' requires a thinking or representing machine to be *in* its data *just as* the eye is in the visual field or writing is in language (in the broad sense)." [216]

Indeed, Jeff Hawkins defines intelligence – and creativity – as the ability to predict the future from past experience, with

---

[215] Lyotard, *The Inhuman* (Stanford: Stanford University Press, 1991), p15
[216] _____, p17.

analogy and metaphor as the primary engine. However, this is hardly a new revelation, considering the extensive work published by George Lakoff and Mark Johnson on the topic of metaphor and how it functions within language[217]. Hawkins gives no explanation of how this process actually operates within the brain. Again, we are thrown back to the interplay of identity and difference discussed in the previous chapter. And again, we find that real, existing human individuals making concrete decisions within a historical context are the defining factor behind what is the same and what is different. No artificial system has even been outlined, let alone defined with sufficient detail for the building of an artificial device capable of this task. Even Lenat realises that the process of learning isn't just absorbing facts, but recreating them anew:

> "Designing more proficient learning programs depends in part on finding ways to tap a source of power at the heart of human intelligence: the ability to understand and reason by analogy."[218]

Nevertheless, Lenat's own Cyc program doesn't address how humans actually perform this feat. Simply recording all the metaphors used in the past (which is what knowledge consists of) says nothing about how we create new ones. Lakoff and Johnson define three traditional modes of analogy: Aristotle's analogies as proportions, analogies based on bodily experience, and analogy as style. In *Metaphors We Live By*, they argue that language about the world starts with the middle of these three, from a basis of body metaphors. So words referring to the body are used to refer to more abstract spatial concepts metaphorically. But these metaphors aren't built up by a mechanistic system, so much as acquired by noticing similarities and differences between the known world and new experiences. This process is organic and individualised, involving judgement.

---

[217] Best epitomized by George Lakoff and Mark Johnson, *Metaphors We Live By* (Chicago and London: The University of Chicago Press, 1980).
[218] D.B. Lenat, "Computer Software for Intelligent Systems," *Scientific American* (September 1984), p204-213.

As Lyotard comments, "In what we call thinking the mind isn't 'directed' but suspended. You don't give it rules. You teach it to receive."[219] We have already stated earlier that the motivation for thinking comes primarily from outside the mind itself – from our animal and emotional needs. But it also comes from the world itself. Jeff Hawkins argues that aspects of experience which don't fit our internal model automatically make us focus upon them. For example, we involuntarily look at a person's physical disability, unless we are used to seeing such things. But this process works far beyond the merely physical, and provides the impetus for thought itself even at the abstract level. If we perceive discontinuities in any mental pattern, this will make us think about the validity of that pattern. It may even force us to reconfigure our conception of the pattern entirely. This is not a mechanical process so much as a destruction and reformation. The reforming creates a new pattern, and may require a different approach each time. It potentially creates new mental structures where none existed before. This gaping void when our patterns are disrupted is what causes our anxiety due to the example which doesn't fit the rule. Artificial intelligence would need to have the same emotional reaction to the novel experience, as it is the physical cue for the creative process. In Lyotard's words,

> "The unthought would have to make your machines uncomfortable, the uninscribed that remains to be inscribed would have to make their memory suffer... Otherwise why would they ever *start* thinking." [220]

However, detecting such discontinuities is not outside the remit of even today's digital systems. Indeed, the popular Search for Extra-Terrestrial Intelligence (SETI) project takes a systematic approach to radio pattern recognition. Using Fast Fourier Transforms, SETI tries to detect a signal from random radio noise, in an attempt to track down alien life outside the Solar System. Similarly, heuristic virus checkers use algorithms to

---

[219] Jean-Francois Lyotard, *The Inhuman* (Stanford: Stanford University Press, 1991), p19.
[220] ____, p20

detect certain types of code within emails, rather than looking for specific viruses. However, whilst both systems can pick up the presence of their targets without needing to know precisely what they are looking for in every respect, their detection abilities are still essentially fixed in kind. The truly original virus, or truly alien life, could well escape its detection – as indeed even the best heuristic anti-virus systems have proven not to be 100 per cent effective. But although a key element of authentic intelligence is clearly missing from any artificial system so far, the artificial variety still has the power to evoke concern. What exactly are we afraid of from our attempts to recreate ourselves synthetically?

Technofear – are computers all-too-human, or not human enough?

The fears we have of our own artificial intelligence technology is best typified by Bill Joy of Sun computers, whose article *Why the future doesn't need us* in *Wired* magazine caused a huge controversy at the time of its publication at the turn of the millennium. Joy states that "Our most powerful 21st century technologies – robotics, genetic engineering, and nanotech – are threatening to make humans an endangered species."[221] However, as we have analysed over the previous chapters, artificial intelligence technology is distinctly flawed as a recreation of the human intellect, and maybe shouldn't even warrant the label "intelligence" at all, as this is an anthropomorphism. Most of it would be better classified as "expert systems", only capable in highly specialised areas. Although, according to Joy, "new technologies like genetic engineering and nanotechnology are giving us the power to remake the world"[222], they don't give us the power to remake the world in our own image so much as in the image we have of ourselves, which is still steeped in metaphysics. The distinction between the two may seem subtle, but there is in fact a whole world of difference hidden behind this nuance.

---

[221] Bill Joy, "Why the future doesn't need us", *Wired*, issue 8.04, April 2000.
[222] Ibid.

Joy cites the Unabomber, as does Ray Kurzweil, to underline the potential pitfalls and responsibilities entailed by the latest technologies:

> "Either of two cases might occur. The machines might be permitted to make all of their own decisions without human oversight, or else human control over the machines might be retained. If the machines are permitted to make all their own decisions, we can't make any conjectures as to the results, because it is impossible to guess how such machines might behave."[223]

This, of course, is assuming computers can make decisions at all – which we have argued no current artificial intelligence technology is capable of. All computers built so far simply perform predetermined calculations on the given data. So they produce the same result when given the same data, every time, or at least the same kind of result. In the last chapter, we will be giving some thought to whether a decision-making machine is possible in the sense we have defined. But for our discussion so far, it suffices to say that if our current technology simply continues to increase in power, we are not in the kind of danger the Unabomber was so worried about. Computers will soon be smarter than us in certain very specific areas, as the most powerful supercomputers already are when playing chess, but a radical shift in how they work will be required for them to exhibit anything like the kind of unfettered ingenuity that humans are capable of. Joy echoes the "grey goo" problem hypothesised by Eric Drexler when he argues,

> "Part of the answer certainly lies in our attitude toward the new – in our bias toward instant familiarity and unquestioning acceptance. Accustomed to living with almost

---

[223] Theodore Kaczynski, "Industrial Society and Its Future (aka the Unabomber Manifesto)", published in the *New York Times* and *Washington Post,* September 19th, 1995.

routine scientific breakthroughs, we have yet
to come to terms with the fact that the most
compelling 21st-century technologies –
robotics, genetic engineering, and
nanotechnology – pose a different threat than
the technologies that have come before.
Specifically, robots, engineered organisms,
and nanobots share a dangerous amplifying
factor: They can self-replicate. A bomb is
blown up only once – but one bot can become
many, and quickly get out of control."[224]

But again, this danger requires the bot in question to have the
ability to make human-like decisions for it to be truly a threat.
We have already gotten used to dumb self-replicators such as
computer viruses, which can be detected and blocked with
simple pattern recognition signatures. As these pieces of code
have no ability to truly mutate – they only alter themselves
according to fixed rules – it is relatively easy to detect them once
they have been discovered. Similarly, even self-replicating
nanobots would have an antidote. Unlike the mutational and
evolutionary ability of biological viruses, the replication of these
machines is limited by their fixed algorithmic basis. Biological
viruses can evolve beyond their antidotes, but no known
computer virus has so far been created with this ability. Even if
it did become possible, because we would have created this self-
copying ability ourselves we could build in safeguards from the
outset, which only deliberate criminal intent would be able to
circumvent.

Like so many who have played a key part in driving the digital
computer revolution, Joy is very optimistic about the potential
future gains in computing power. This optimism is not misplaced
when it comes to the increasing ability of these systems to
perform the tasks they are currently already capable of, only
faster and more efficiently than ever before. But simple

---

[224] Bill Joy, "Why the future doesn't need us", *Wired*, issue 8.04, April 2000.

optimism and faith in Moore's Law[225] doesn't address the sea change in technology which will be required to give artificial intelligence the kind of abilities we have singled out in our discussions of artistic creativity – if these abilities can be recreated synthetically at all. Joy states that:

> "because of the recent rapid and radical progress in molecular electronics – where individual atoms and molecules replace lithographically drawn transistors – and related nanoscale technologies, we should be able to meet or exceed the Moore's law rate of progress for another 30 years. By 2030, we are likely to be able to build machines, in quantity, a million times as powerful as the personal computers of today – sufficient to implement the dreams of Kurzweil and Moravec."[226]

We have already discussed the flaws in Kurzweil's bullish confidence in the power of his "Law of Accelerating Returns" earlier in this chapter. Joy asks "How soon could such an intelligent robot be built?", and answers that "The coming advances in computing power seem to make it possible by 2030. And once an intelligent robot exists, it is only a small step to a robot species – to an intelligent robot that can make evolved copies of itself."[227] He is clearly expecting a miracle in computer science. The paradigm shift required could be just around the corner, but just as the revolutions in relativity and quantum mechanics could not be predicted before they had actually happened, there's no clear timeline of when (or what) will be required for truly intelligent machines. All we have so far is the kind of conjecture with which will be concluding Chapter 6.

---

[225] This is the famous observation by Intel co-founder Gordon Moore that the complexity of integrated circuits was doubling every two years. This was first published in "Cramming more components onto integrated circuits", *Electronics Magazine* (19 April 1965).
[226] Bill Joy, "Why the future doesn't need us", *Wired*, issue 8.04, April 2000.
[227] Ibid.

Where Joy does conform with the view we have traced here is in his belief that the current trends in technology could leave humanity high and dry. Even if artificial intelligence is aimed at extending human mental abilities, he argues:

> "But if we are downloaded into our technology, what are the chances that we will thereafter be ourselves or even human? It seems to me far more likely that a robotic existence would not be like a human one in any sense that we understand, that the robots would in no sense be our children, that on this path our humanity may well be lost."[228]

Certainly, if we think that the products of our current artificial intelligence technology are meant to supersede us, as Kurzweil does, humanity will indeed be lost. With their basis in our metaphysical view of ourselves, these systems threaten to replace living human beings with lifeless instruments based on our own idealised self conception. However, Schirmacher expresses surprise that our fear of our own creations doesn't ring alarm bells that not so much our machines, but our image of ourselves could be at fault:

> "How reluctant we really are to part with the traditional image of man, despite our pretence at being severe critics of subjectivity, is proven by our fierce resistance when computers and robots are called 'flesh of our flesh'. Ironically, this resistance intensifies the closer the cybernetic machines come to approximating those human characteristics which we have reserved for ourselves alone: thought, imagination, learning from mistakes."[229]

---

[228] Ibid.

[229] Wolfgang Schirmacher, "Eco-sophia: the artist of life", *Research in Philosophy and Technology 9: Ethics and Technology*, ed Carl Mitcham (JAI Press: Greenwhich/London 1989).

Artificial intelligence systems can only be viewed as a human product. Since we are the ones creating them, what else could they be? So if they are destined to make us extinct, they must clearly be a sign of our own death wish rather than themselves being at fault. The creation of nuclear weapons in parallel with nuclear power stations reveals the two sides to most human technological advancements. But the fact that we even consider creating machines to replace ourselves entirely says far more than our continuing inability to actually create those machines. It could tell us the whole focus of the technological drive is potentially against life itself.

But does that mean all attempts to recreate human intelligence artificially are equally life-threatening? So far, we have discussed how current computer technology is based on a metaphysical, incomplete view of ourselves. In the next chapter, we will turn to a few more arguments showing how this project is doomed to failure. But then we will speculate on some areas which could lead to a more human-like artificial intelligence, and ask whether these areas could provide a closer approximation to human intelligence, perhaps with the ability to create truly original works of art.

Chapter 6
The soul of a computer

It has become clear over the last five chapters that it's impossible to discuss the question of computers making art without having to address the fundamental questions of artificial intelligence. As we have discovered, artistic creativity is one of the human activities which is hardest to conceptualise – and therefore even harder to compute. Indeed, Kant called the experience of beauty a judgement without concept[230]. We have argued from philosophical points of view that the origin of art lies outside systematic algorithmic computation. In a similar way, Roger Penrose has attempted to use Gödel's incompleteness theorems to show that consciousness goes beyond a bunch of mathematical algorithms[231]. Penrose has argued that as it's impossible to solve all mathematical problems within the scope of an existing mathematical theory, a simple mathematical algorithm for the mind will never exist. Gödel's most famous first incompleteness theory states that:

> "For any formal theory in which basic arithmetical facts are provable, it is possible to construct an arithmetical statement which, if the theory is consistent, is true but not provable or refutable in the theory."[232]

In other words, proving such statements requires stepping outside the formal mathematical system, in much the same way as we have argued that creating art requires stepping outside rational thought and logical systems, even if they are derived from a study of all the art which has ever gone before. The fundamental truth in art is evident, but by its nature goes beyond

---

[230] Kant, Immanuel. *The Critique of Judgement.* Oxford: Oxford University Press, 1952.

[231] In Roger Penrose *The Emperor's New Mind* (Oxford: Oxford University Press, 1999) and *Shadows of the Mind* (Oxford: Oxford University Press, 1996).

[232] K. Gödel, "Some basic theorems on the foundations of mathematics and their implications", *Collected Works, Vol. III. Unpublished Essays and Lectures*, ed S. Feferman et al, (New York: Oxford University Press, 1995), p304-323.

previous art history. Representational art is something which existing computer systems could (and do) replicate in a convincing way, for it involves relatively functional transformations of incoming sensual data. This is the kind of algebraic calculation computers were designed to perform, although it's really only a few steps away from the chemical processes involved in photography. But abstract art is a different matter, for it represents a more rarefied essence of the artistic process. In fact, although it's a purer form of art devoid of obvious utility, abstract art merely shows how even representational art cannot be understood as mere representation. The subjective element is still an important factor in defining where the "artistry" comes from, and this is distinctly lacking in a direct algorithmic transformation. An artwork expresses something beyond what it directly represents, and our appreciation of it points in multiple directions. Lyotard argues that: "On the subject of taste, the critique should and must support two apparently contradictory propositions: taste is a singular, subjective judgement that does not make use of any concept; taste is a judgement that lays claim to universality and necessity, which are categories of the understanding, ie, the faculty of concepts." [233] In contrast, the programmer who thought up an art-creating transformation in the first place has shown creativity in the formula's inception, but the machine which performs it over and over again is merely mechanically reproducing its effect – it operates purely with the faculty of predefined concepts. It is not showing creativity itself, and not expressing anything beyond the programmer's original code. The computer user is still required to inject original expression into the mechanical process, by choosing which predefined technique to use at a given time.

When the artists discussed in the introduction use their so-called art-creating machines, what is really the artwork? Is it the output of the machine, or the machine itself – or maybe even the combination of the two? Each one of these art-creation systems could make a great example of the Freudo-Lacanian death drive

---

[233] Jean-Francois Lyotard, *Lessons on the Analytic of the Sublime* (Stanford: Stanford University Press, 1994), p207.

– the artist committing suicide and handing over their own task of creation to their machines – except for the fact that our focus remains on the artist as well as their mechanised creation. But this could also be a failure to hear the resounding message from these machines, that perhaps as soon as we've systematised the process in a particular art, we still fail to grasp the essence of art itself, as Nancy argues in *The Muses*. According to Nancy, in every species of a genus, the one thing missing is the species which embodies the genus itself in all cases. So the definitive essence of art remains a gaping void, despite each one of us having a prototypical artwork in mind. Art-creating machines could pose the strongest question of our computational technology tied to enframing, and our metaphysics which makes an object of the subject. These machines fail in the attempt at modelling the essence of art, instead simulating the output of a particular genre of art. They could be an example of just how alienated we are from our own life processes – or they could simply be new life techniques there to serve us when we want.

Art-creating machines, considered solely on their own merits, fail to take into account the leap involved in creativity, like all attempts at artificial consciousness thus far. By its very nature, the act of creation transcends the rules and reasons which have gone before. As Slavoj Zizek argues, "Is not such a suspension of the 'principle of sufficient reason(s)', however, the very definition of the *act*?"[234]. The end result may be systematic, as it is in technological innovation, but that system remains unknown until the act has occurred. The process of its inception is clearly anti-systematic. Although our modernist, rationalist culture is based on the idea that decisions are made by calculating the options so that the choice is an obvious logical derivation, in fact "every decision ... bases itself on something not mastered, something concealed, confusing; else it would never be a decision."[235] If we were to find a system behind decision, humanity's species-long mission would be accomplished and time would cease to exist. All decisions would logically follow

[234] Slavoj Zizek, *The Ticklish Subject* (London: Verso, 1999), p388.
[235] *The origin of the work of art* in Martin Heidegger, *Basic Writings* (London: Routledge, 1993), p180.

from the environmental circumstances, and the mistakes and experimentation which characterise human development would no longer be necessary, as the machines could do it all for us at increasing speed. The belief that this is possible, or even desirable, is a result of our Enframing by our own technology, and only further creative thinking can get us out of this trap. In turn, Enframing is the modern end result of Being, the final manifestation of the metaphysical belief. For, as Heidegger argues, "Being, as the essence of technology, has adapted itself into Enframing"[236] But this is no eternal trap, as thought itself offers an escape route. Again, according to Heidegger,

> "Language is the primal dimension within which man's essence is first able to correspond at all to Being and its claim, and, in corresponding, to belong to Being. This primal corresponding, expressly carried out, is thinking. Through thinking, we first learn to dwell in the realm in which there comes to pass the restorative surmounting of the destining of Being, the surmounting of Enframing."[237]

Art is the purest form of thinking taking place, of the discovery of truth as aletheia. So, art itself offers an antidote to the metaphysical programme of Enframing, which is now epitomised in the attempts to create machines with human intelligence. Far from being just another human endeavour which will one day be understood by the marching theories of scientific discovery, art offers the clearest argument that science has its limits when applied to humanity. The human will to generate beauty transcends its own systematisation.

---

[236] *The Turning* in Martin Heidegger, *The Question Concerning Technology* (New York: Harper Torchbooks, 1977), p38.
[237] ____, p41.

March of the positivists

Despite the many arguments against it, many continue to argue that true artificial intelligence will be possible this century. At the end of *The Age of Spiritual Machines*, Ray Kurzweil suggests that combining recursive programming (the lambda calculus of Keene and Church described in Chapter 3), neural nets and evolutionary algorithms could lead towards computers displaying artificial intelligence. Alternatively, in his book *On Intelligence*, Jeff Hawkins argues that the human intellect is characterised by memory-based prediction based on pattern recognition. Hawkins's hypothesis is at least based on study of the human brain, in particular the neocortex, rather than simply assuming that an idealised digital technology can mimic the organic workings of the mind with little reference to empirical evidence. However, his definition of intelligence as memory-based prediction using past experience is still very instrumental in its conception. All the examples he gives are of goal-oriented problem solving, where the precise ends of each action can be clearly formulated. There is no mention of situations where actions occur without the end being obvious in advance – as we have argued is consistently the case with artistic creativity.

Neither of these theories take into account the singular quality of the experience of the world we have described as the basis of art, and consciousness itself. All of these so-called intelligent systems base their decisions on past experience, without the ability to go beyond memory or systematic learning processes. The active, wilful aspect of the human has been sideline, indicating that these artificial intelligence theorists are themselves stuck in the Enframed mindset we have described elsewhere. That's not to say that their theories won't result in the creation of useful machines which are highly likely to enhance human life. As Schirmacher argues, "The recent death-bringing technology is, though in a totally distorted way, the selfsame life-sustaining technology of man conceived of originally." [238]

---

[238] Wolfgang Schirmacher, "From the phenomenon to the event of technology", *Philosophy and Technology*, ed F Rapp (Reidel: Dordrecht 1983), *Boston Studies in the Philosophy of Science 80.*

But their intended purpose will be missing a crucial element of human intelligence, because "Through the cybernetic machine, in the end, man and machine will be brought together in a synthesis of a work of art honouring the artificialness of both – but missing the link to life and to our nature." [239]

To be fair on Hawkins, he explicitly states that he is not hoping to create entire human beings, as we have already noted in the previous chapter. He just wants to use the knowledge of how the neocortex works to develop machines capable of much more human-like tasks than current Von Neumann machines are able to perform. For example, Hawkins envisages systems capable of driving vehicles automatically, or a global weather prediction system using sensors placed all over the globe. He also clearly understands that to have full human understanding, an artificial intelligence would have to experience life as a human being – with a fully operational body, plus all the physical and emotional baggage that entails. However, as he himself points out, the neocortex is not the only portion of the brain which is involved in our ability to form memories. Although there is much experimental evidence that the neocortex is the home of well established memories, the initial acquisition and upkeep of memory has been extensively linked to the hippocampus. This very old part of the brain is particularly prominent in primates and Cetacean sea mammals. So merely unravelling the workings of neocortex might prove fruitless for the wider question of creating machines with more holistically human-like intelligence and initiative, even if the discoveries made assist the development of increasingly capable computer systems. Perhaps this research will explain how memories persist, but it may not tell us how they get there in the first place. This yet again brings us back to the central theme of our argument. Although art has been our main vehicle of discussion, we have inferred that the arbitrary wilfulness involved is as much a part of everyday life as it is of rarefied artistic genius. Without this ability to "make judgement calls" which go beyond past experience, an artificial intelligence will find itself unable to deal with numerous

---

[239] Ibid.

situations which simply don't adequately fit anything which went before. Hawkins' neocortex-based devices would be like Alzheimer's sufferers, unable to remember recent events, and possibly slowly forgetting some of the more distant ones as well. Additional research on how the hippocampus works could prove helpful, but its workings are one of the greatest areas of dispute in neuroscience.[240] Also, unlike the neocortex, which is far larger in homo sapiens sapiens than other species, the human hippocampus is far from unique. In other words, it may well be our ability to store complex abstract models of the world which makes us special in the animal kingdom, but the creative ability founding that understanding is not so unusual. Rats can learn their ways round mazes too, and even dogs can behave as if they have a sense of humour. Perhaps this is why technology, which is an extension of our neocortical ability, already feels neither like part of ourselves nor simply another part of the material world. As Wolfgang Schirmacher comments,

> "Machine technology however exhibits the characteristics of an indisputable autonomy; its functioning obeys an intrinsic law, is clearly automatic. This in no way makes technology the subject; it means technology is apparently no longer adequately describable within the customary subject-object relationship." [241]

The argument here splits into two. On the one hand, art and the intuitive intelligence it exemplifies potentially cannot be simulated without taking into account aspects of the brain which are not uniquely human. But, on the other hand, the systems theorists such as Kurzweil and Hawkins propose, and indeed all

---

[240] For example, in "Evidence for semantic learning in profound amnesia: An investigation with patient H.M", *Hippocampus*, Volume 14, Issue 4, p417-425, Gail O'Kane, Elizabeth A. Kensinger, and Suzanne Corkin present clinical evidence that new semantic memories can be formed by a human being whose hippocampi have been removed.

[241] Wolfgang Schirmacher, "From the phenomenon to the event of technology", *Philosophy and Technology*, ed F Rapp (Reidel: Dordrecht 1983), *Boston Studies in the Philosophy of Science 80.*

of our computational technologies so far, do in fact represent and embody uniquely human traits. Again, in Schirmacher's words,

> "If man should free himself from the conception of his being unique, and should come to comprehend personality and morality as the improvised solutions of an 'imperfect being' (Gehlen), he would be astounded at how closely machines approximate the self-image of man, how they are more human than humans."[242]

One of the most interesting discoveries in Hawkins' work is how the brain amalgamates input from the various senses. Beyond a certain point up the hierarchical structure of the brain, sensory input becomes abstract patterns, and there is no differentiation whether the input originated as light, sound, or tactile response. Most significantly of all, memory of both spatial and temporal patterns are stored in the same homogeneous way, according to research cited by Hawkins. So the temporal patterns in music and the spatial ones in the visual arts come together in a common repository. Similarly, fresh experiences of similar patterns and their memory trigger activity in the same regions – so the brain registers the smell of a flower and the memory of that smell in a similar way. This complements well our arguments in Chapter 2, following Nancy, that before the arts there was just art, and that only in material expression does the separation of each individual art form have any relevance. The underlying creative process across all types of art starts with the same ill-defined abstract conception. So, for example, when Siegfried Zielinski makes a distinction between time-based media and genres such as film, the underlying sensual effect is not as greatly differentiated as he would imply. Zielinski's concept of time-based media underlines artworks which play on multiple senses at once, both spatially and temporally, and calls for a creative process which is a symbiosis of man and machine. But it would appear that for the brain itself, all the dimensions are one

---

[242] Ibid.

already. So although Nietzsche and Schopenhauer attribute music with the highest level of purity, as the closest art to will itself, this is not something inherent in music itself. The absence of the spatial in music does not give it this purity, but its non-representational abstraction, which is a historical and cultural product. Any art operating through any of the senses without clear representational intention could exhibit the same wilfulness, as indeed our examples from 20th century abstraction in the visual arts underline. But prior to that time, music was the only art which eschewed representational intent.

Nowadays, we live in a post-MTV world, where the abstraction of the music video has created the most commercially successful examples of non-representational time-based artistry. The abstraction of music has been allied with visual content which may have some direct semantic element, but primarily works at a raw level of seduction, in the sense used by Jean Baudrillard. These hyper-technologised media works represent "cybernetic art" in its most comfortable realisation yet. As Schirmacher argues, "The technical art-work process corresponds to the purest form of process. [] ...the cybernetic technologies make possible the rendering of true occurrence, and not wilful dominance by man." [243] It is no irony that the music video has become the surprising heir to the abstract film experiments of the early 20th century. Indeed, the shamelessly synthetic quality of these hybrid media forms presaged the cybernetic culture which is now becoming the norm. Not only is the music video neither pure music nor pure film, it is also both content and advertisement for that content. As well as offering a multimedia experience, the music video also represents the total commercialisation of culture, where it is no longer possible to separate the product of creativity from its commoditisation and exploitation. Benjamin's mechanical reproduction of artworks has reached full maturity, and "we, as the 'artificial', as technical beings by nature, are inevitably destroying the pre-existent natural order." [244]

---

[243] Ibid.
[244] Ibid.

But the music video is already a part of a previous era in technical culture, where the artwork was enlisted as part of the industrialisation of media. This "broadcast" era is in fast decline, as witnessed by the rapid decrease in viewer numbers for the most popular TV programmes, or radio listeners. Indeed, Lev Manovich has argued that the term artwork may no longer be appropriate for the cybernetic creations of the computer era, instead suggesting they be called "media objects"[245], and hinting at the far more explicitly active role the user now takes. The computer game or social networking website is a distinctly different form to the music video, and emphasises our participation in the creation of our own realities. This is yet another sign of man's conquering of nature and the real, and "We must learn to live with the realization that artificiality is the nature of man, and that technology, in all its so uncommonly diverse forms, is the realized, cosmic mode of being peculiar to our nature and which must be further perfected. Technology is the human way of corresponding to the universe." [246] The popular media of the past few centuries were passed down from central organisations to the masses. But, with the arrival of the Internet and community-based media phenomena such as MySpace, YouTube and Facebook, the masses are gaining much more control over the popularity of media content, and shaping their own social reality as a result. This is perfectly in line with man's erasure of reality via technology. Once upon a time, "The substance of things, not techniques, seemed to decide about our life up to now. But in truth, only techniques are real and the 'substances' are our irresponsible projections." [247]

A conceptualisation of human intelligence as a unified system in common to all humans would seem at odds with this many-to-many cultural context. Like a broadcast TV channel, this would be to project an idealised image of humanity onto itself, instead

[245] Lev Manovich, *The Language of New Media* (Cambridge, Massachussetts: The MIT Press, 2001).
[246] Wolfgang Schirmacher, "From the phenomenon to the event of technology", *Philosophy and Technology*, ed F Rapp (Reidel: Dordrecht 1983), *Boston Studies in the Philosophy of Science 80.*
[247] Ibid.

of letting the true differences reveal themselves. A salient feature of the Internet age is that humans are interacting with other humans more than ever, rather than passively consuming the industrially reproduced artefacts of centralised media conglomerates. They are appropriating, re-editing, and redistributing the produce of the established media at will. Instead of "one size fits all", Heidegger's "existential philosophy of the human race" would make a much more appropriate approach – "an ethics of 'releasement' (Gelassenheit): thought and action unfettered by prepossession – endurance to resist the demands of the day – mortal action: mindful of posterity and nature alike – personally assumed responsibility for the whole rejection of anthropocentrism and the practice of an ascetic reason."[248] In other words, the image of the human must be replaced by living, ever-changing humans. Nothing is sacred, copyrights included.

Towards the possibility of AI

Many of our arguments have been against the possibility of computers making art, even computers based on radically different technology than our current digital systems. But the lion's share of criticism has been focused on the Enframing inherent in our current, information-based approach to computing. This self-fulfilling prophesy of technology shuts out an important aspect of creativity and intelligence. However, in part this is because even technology such as the evolutionary systems, recursive algorithms and neural nets suggested by Kurzweil are still founded in the Newtonian paradigm, where end results are determined by initial criteria. Few mainstream AI theories have attempted to think in terms of the relativist, quantum and non-Euclidian geometric paradigms which came to fore at the beginning of the 20th century. The beginnings of new directions of enquiry are emerging. Nagel considers that: "It may be possible to approach the gap between subjective and objective

---

[248] Wolfgang Schirmacher, "Eco-sophia: the artist of life", *Research in Philosophy and Technology 9: Ethics and Technology*, ed Carl Mitcham (JAI Press: Greenwhich/London 1989).

from another direction. Setting aside temporarily the relation between the mind and the brain, we can pursue a more objective understanding of the mental in its own right." [249] However, he doesn't provide very clear directions of how such an objective language of the subjective could be formed. Roger Penrose has argued that quantum mechanical functions could lie at the heart of neurons[250], as a way to explain his hypothesis that digital computers couldn't even be used to model human intelligence adequately, let alone supply the hardware for a new artificial intelligence. But this doesn't really preclude the possibility of AI altogether, just the chance that current digital systems could develop consciousness. Computers are themselves evolving in this direction anyway. As integrated circuit miniaturisation meets the atomic level, quantum uncertainty effects will start to play a part. Indeed, the use of quantum effects as a form of computing has been talked about for some years, and even been shown to work. Isaac Chang of Los Alamos National Laboratory and MIT's Neil Gershenfeld have demonstrated working quantum computing using the carbon atoms in the alanine molecule, although their system was only capable of adding one and one at the time of writing. Penrose suggests that brains operate at this quantum level, and the uncertainty could be a contributory factor to the sense of consciousness. His theories have been further developed by Stuart Hameroff MD, who argues that the microtubules in the brain contain elements small enough for quantum phenomena to occur, and has coined the term 'quantum consciousness' to represent these ideas.

If Penrose and Hameroff are right, and the human brain does have smaller functional elements than neurons which work at the quantum level, a number of strange effects could follow on. For example, a "quantum entanglement" effect has been demonstrated experimentally. This is where two "entangled" quantum particles remain connected no matter what the distance. When one particle is prepared with one quantum state, another

[249] Thomas Nagel, *What is it like to be a bat?* (*The Philosophical Review* LXXXIII, 4 (October 1974): 435-50).

[250] Roger Penrose, *The Emperor's New Mind* (Oxford: Oxford University Press, 1999).

entangled particle will be recorded with the same state, no matter the distance separating them. This is in direct contradiction to quantum uncertainty, according to which it should be impossible to predict in advance the exact state of a particle. Quantum entanglement has been demonstrated conclusively by Dr Nicolas Gisin at the University of Geneva, using the behaviour of photons. If similar effects are occurring naturally in the human brain, then this could give a hard scientific explanation for "spooky" phenomena such as sensing a distant relative's death. But it could also shed light on the everyday intuitive sense of compassion. Whilst this theory is clearly very farfetched and unlikely to be borne out by extensive research, we have provided it here as an example of the kind of recently discovered physical effects which could contribute to the mysterious way the human brain operates. Quantum entanglement has been experimentally shown to exist, and it is just one of a number of subatomic phenomena which could render the workings of the mind far more complex than has been assumed. At a more basic level, quantum-mechanical events are considered truly random, something which could contribute the sense of freedom experienced by conscious beings. If such quantum effects are discovered to play a significant role in neurology, it would entirely refute the ability of any technologies proposed thus far to produce artificial intelligence. And if systems were produced with such knowledge, by their very nature they would be unpredictable. But that is exactly in line with human beings, and why artificial intelligence has provoked so much fear, expressed in movies from *2001* to *The Matrix* and *The Terminator*. After all, we find it nearly impossible to trust each other, so a physically more powerful machine being similarly unpredictable is a potential worst nightmare.

Quantum effects or not, there is plenty of evidence that something unpredictable exists in human thought, with art providing the most obvious example. There are a number of arguments which could be levelled against this. One is the simple denial that art is in fact original in the way that we have described, and states that it's just the product of a systematic process just like any other human faculty like vision. This argument is akin to the denial of Qualia and consciousness we discussed in a previous chapter. Another counter-argument has already been touched upon in Chapter 2, and refutes the nature of art we've described here, denying that modern abstract art is in fact art. This politically conservative view reinstates the mimetic quality of representational art as its main function, although it would still have trouble explaining the subjective interpretation involved in even the most straight-laced portrait. At the most basic level, however, is an argument related to the distinction made by Kant in his *Critique of Judgment* between the beautiful and that which is merely pleasant to the senses. The beautiful makes claims to universality, whereas the pleasant is simply subjective. It could be argued that art is actually just pleasant, and its claims to universality are a myth propagated by the pretentious and others with a vested interested in continuing that myth.

Still, in line with what we have already seen in many of the grand claims for artificial intelligence thus far, using current systems to produce independent art-creating computers is doomed to failure, even when aimed at generating merely pleasant works. Whilst the experiments in evolutionary algorithms of Eno, Latham and Sims are interesting, they don't really point towards machines becoming creative in their own right. The human artist is still very much in residence. Indeed, at the time of writing the era of interest in the artistic output from such systems has already subsided. The range of possibilities from art creation machines may be statistically limitless, but the human taste which is still required to decide whether any of the options presented are worth anything remains distinctly fickle. Since the systems aren't capable of true originality in themselves, requiring further programming or innovative usage to achieve novel results, their output starts to look the same after experiencing a few examples. So the whole concept goes out of fashion. Even if the algorithms mean that the output is never actually the same, that's no guarantee that it will have the characteristics required of an artwork. Without the human contribution, it could remain at the level of mere noise – a meaningless ground rather than significant figure.

The randomness of nature has been a focus of attention in the 1980s and 1990s. Chaos theory (and the fractal mathematics of complex numbers underlying it) has engendered considerable interest, for its ability to resemble the minute variations found in the real world. But it's still a simulation, and although the algorithms have found useful applications in areas such as image compression, there's no evidence that the complex polynomial functions behind Mandelbrot and Julia sets really bear any direct relation to the more arbitrary activities of human thought. Indeed, we have already discussed how Roger Penrose has used Gödel's incompleteness theory to show that human thought processes cannot consist purely of mathematical algorithms. Another option would be to use random numbers to generate unpredictable results, a capability which most computers already have. However, these so-called random numbers are just a pre-defined string kept in memory and followed sequentially. These pseudorandom numbers are usually created by a deterministic algorithm, rather than produced on the fly. They don't pass statistical tests of randomness. Hardware random number generators do exist, based on microscopic phenomena, particularly quantum behaviour. But this would bring us back to our hypothesis that there is a quantum effect occurring somewhere within the workings of human consciousness.

From replacement to inclusion

We have argued consistently against current digital technology becoming sentient, and also that the attempt to make it so is the pinnacle of the metaphysical programme in Western thought. But this does not necessarily lead to the conclusion that the use of this kind of technology in artistic activity is pointless. Instead, the development of ever more complex systems expands the range of options available to the artist – so long as they are viewed as an augmentation of human ability, rather than its complete replacement. One of the criticisms often levelled at the use of new technology as a democratisation and liberation of artistic endeavour is that the end results are amateurish. From desktop publishing, to photo retouching, to home MIDI music making, the cultural establishment and its supporters attack the application of new technology, arguing that it unleashes banal creativity in people who don't have the talent required to "make the grade" using the pre-existing means. But this is clearly as much a fear of a change in the social order as it is valid critique. So long as technology is integrated into life, rather than pitted against it, technology should not be feared. This is a clearly different attitude to Luddite technofear, as Schirmacher explains:

> "We should understand and respond to the fact that a fundamental shift in the whole historical process is approaching, a shift which is, in a phenomenological sense, self generated. We could call the new state of affairs 'history without metaphysics', which would be, couched in traditional language, the basis for a renewed 'practical philosophy', as suggested by Gerard Raulet. But this philosophy would have to be neither anthropocentric nor Eurocentric, but would have to depart altogether from the metaphysical conception of a centre." [251]

New technology always brings with it a dehumanising danger. Continuing to produce technology as an idealised version of ourselves runs this risk. Any assumption that we completely know what we are will unquestionably fail to see something important about being human. Nietzsche describes it thus: "The pride connected with knowing and sensing lies like a blinding fog over the eyes and senses of men, thus deceiving them concerning the value of existence." [252] Modern computer systems are an offshoot of our metaphysical image of human thought as an algorithmic computational system. And, as Schirmacher argues, "If we proceed along the way of metaphysics only

---

[251] Wolfgang Schirmacher, "The End of Metaphysics", *SOCIAL SCIENCE INFORMATION 23*, 3 (1984), p603-609.
[252] Friedrich Nietzsche, *On Truth and Lies in a Nonmoral Sense* (unpublished, 1873), p1.

artefacts will survive, not human beings and objects."[253] But whilst Enframing is inherent in technology, according to Heidegger, the realisation of this fact offers the ability to transcend the intended purpose of technology and use it for different ends. After all, Nietzsche considered some untruths necessary for the continuation of life. Indeed, even science itself sits on unstable ground, according to Kuhn. Every paradigm of scientific truth is only valid until its refutation arrives. Those with vested interests in the old way of thinking may cling to the past, but once they die their dogma dies with them, to be replaced with the updated view. So every current scientific theory will eventually be superseded, and should be considered the best we have found so far rather than absolute truth. In the same way, instrumental technology can take a valid place in the artistic process, so long as its limitations are taken into consideration and it is not treated as sacred. "'Once we have words for something, we have gone beyond it', reads a maxim from *The Twilight of the Idols*, descriptive and self-assured. This having 'gone beyond' sets the keynote of an artificial perception."[254]

In many ways, the debates surrounding artificial intelligence are purely academic. Despite the pessimism of theorists such as Bill Joy, or the optimism of Ray Kurzweil and Hans Moravec, the chances are we will not be rendered obsolete by faster and faster computers. As has been argued here, we are still missing many of the vital theories about how human intelligence works, and until we discover what they are, our machines will only simulate a small subset of our mental abilities – and there will always be aspects of human existence which remain mysterious. However, there are dangers involved as our attempts close in on some of the important milestones, especially if we falsely believe we have created true artificial humans when all we have created are good likenesses. Giving our machines superior mental faculties than our own, and then imbuing them with the originality of

---

[253] Ibid.

[254] Wolfgang Schirmacher, *Cloning Humans with Media: Impermanence and Imperceptible Perfection*, http://www.egs.edu/faculty/schirmacher/schirmacher-cloning-humans-with-media.html (2000).

thought that is a key ingredient of being human, doesn't necessarily entail that such machines will act in our favour. Just as people can choose a life of crime, there's no guarantee that an AI would have compassion for humanity. It is our responsibility to ensure that our machines remain enhancements to our lives, rather than its destructors. Just as limits are required on our usage of nuclear technology, artificial intelligence needs strict control – and this goes far beyond Asimov's Three Laws of Robotics[255]. After all, why do we need to recreate ourselves artificially when we can do this so well biologically? It makes far more sense to view artificial intelligence as an enhancement of what we already have. We must put ourselves as living beings back in the picture, rather than taking a snapshot of ourselves and making this the defining portrait. As Schirmacher has pointed out, Nietzsche's philosophy of eternal self-revaluation of all values is just as important in the decentralised Internet age as it was in the colonial era during which it was written:

> "But the right of the human individual on the other hand to be 'human-uniquely-human' of one's own strength, and to take responsibility for one's own world as 'primordial poetry' corresponds to Nietzsche's vision of 'self-potentiation'." [256]

Indeed, far from going against the philosophy of Nietzsche, the most significant scientific discoveries of the 20th century underline the impossibility of knowing the physical world without human participation. As we discussed in chapter 5,

---

[255] Introduced in Asimov's 1942 short story "Runaround", the Laws state the following:
1. A robot may not injure a human being or, through inaction, allow a human being to come to harm.
2. A robot must obey orders given it by human beings except where such orders would conflict with the First Law.
3. A robot must protect its own existence as long as such protection does not conflict with the First or Second Law.

Later, Asimov added the "Zeroth law": a robot may not harm humanity, or, by inaction, allow humanity to come to harm. This was introduced later on in the internal chronology of the series.
[256] Ibid.

quantum mechanics itself makes the observer centrally important. At the subatomic level, quantum uncertainty shows that you cannot predict the precise result of an experiment in advance – only human observation can reveal this. The best that can be calculated is the average result, or the probability of a given result. At this level, the universe is not mathematically determined, only statistically approximated. Human observation is an absolute requirement for knowledge. Similarly, special relativity makes the passage of time relative to the viewer, not something knowable from an impartial universal perspective.

Despite these discoveries, deterministic computers are not only the current folk way of thinking, with people talking about "multi-tasking" as if they are themselves digital machines running multiple applications. They are also the metaphor guiding most of our current scientific theory in other areas. DNA is seen as a digital computerised system, with living beings simply reduced to little computers executing DNA programs just as our desktop PCs run their software. Environmental conditions make the results unpredictable, but only because we don't have all the information. Even in the work of evolutionary experts such as Richard Dawkins, mutation is taken for granted as our DNA executes its code, rather than being seen as the fundamental mystery behind the life process itself. The implications of the non-Euclidean scientific discoveries of Einstein and Heisenberg have not made their way into these areas sufficiently yet. Living beings are still seen as statistical species rather than a myriad evolving singularities.

In the perspectivism we described in chapter 4, the one universal belief left is that there is the same reality underlying our differing perspectives. This is a key distinction. It has to be the same reality, rather than lots of different ones. No two living beings will ever see that reality in exactly the same way, because "[thought] can do one thing and its opposite, present an object in a finite way and conceive an object as actually infinite." [257]

---

[257] Jean-Francois Lyotard, *Lessons on the Analytic of the Sublime* (Stanford: Stanford University Press, 1994), p150.

But this is where science still needs a religion of sorts, as there has to be a leap of faith that despite our differing perspectives, we all live in the same underlying world. But other than that, finding absolutely common ground between all humans, at least enough to model a generalised intelligence artificially, seems a futile endeavour. There is no absolutely common ground because there is no central value in human life, as Schirmacher argues:

> "The artistic will to artificial life, analyzed by Heidegger as the 'will to will', has no aim, and is tautological in structure. Consciously anthropomorphic, this realization of will seeks its fulfilment as fulfilment – not other, only fulfilment of itself (albeit in the identity of difference of self and otherness)." [258]

But to understand this as a form of nihilism is to miss the point. It does not make the striving for value in artistic creativity a lost cause, or a chasing of non-existent dreams. Those who believe man will be transcended by machine are also those likely to dismiss the abstract art examples given in earlier chapters as mere chimera – not real art, just the empty pretence of a self-aggrandising art community. This is a key consideration, as it reveals the political rather than merely technical dimension to our argument. Those who believe these abstract examples are art do so at a level which cannot be explained in the exhaustive technical terms required by their detractors, for it reaches towards a sublime which transcends conceptualisation even as it is embodied in a physical work. The question is therefore why this should mean that their beliefs don't exist, or have no relevance to the development of intelligent machines.

There is a strong belief amongst AI evangelists that our machines won't just go beyond us by exceeding our abilities in mere quantity terms – simply beating us at our own game (starting with chess…). Instead, they will change the game

---

[258] Ibid.

entirely, and see the world in a much more complex way, utterly beyond our understanding. For example, Moravec argues that "Our mind children, able to manipulate their own substance and structure at the finest levels, will probably greatly transcend our narrow notions of what is."[259] However, although we all want the best for our children, what we really want is for our own conscious lives never to end. And since we must die, passing as much as possible of ourselves onto another generation both genetically and culturally is the next best thing. Future technology will continue to increase our life expectancy, giving us longer to realise our creative wishes. In this context, the drive to develop machines which can replicate and eventually replace our creative abilities seems ludicrous. The question is therefore not whether computers can make art, but why we would want them to do so in the first place. Instead of rendering ourselves obsolete, we would be better off concentrating on using digital technology as another part of our existing creative ability, in the full realisation that there will always be uniquely human characteristics which we cannot fully describe and replicate.

---

[259] Hans Moravec, *Robot* (Oxford: Oxford University Press, 1999), p208.

Bibliography

Adorno, Theodor and Horkheimer, Max. *Dialectic of Enlightenment*. New York: Verso, 1997.

Barthes, Roland. *A Roland Barthes Reader*. London: Vintage, 1993.

_____. *Camera Lucida*. London: Vintage, 1993.

Baudrillard, Jean. *Selected Writings*. Stanford: Stanford University Press, 1988.

Benjamin, Walter. *Illuminations*. New York: Schocken Books, 1969.

Bois, Yves-Alain. *Painting as Model*. Cambridge, Massachussetts: The MIT Press, 1990.

Bois, Yves-Alain and Krauss, Rosalind E. *Formless: A Users Guide*. New York: Zone Books, 2000.

Broks, Paul. *Into the Silent Land*. London: Atlantic Books, 2003.

Burke, Edmund. *A Philosophical Enquiry*. Oxford: Oxford University Press, 1990.

Dawkins, Richard. *Climbing Mount Improbable*. London: Penguin Books, 1997.

Deleuze, Gilles. *The Fold: Leibniz and the Baroque*. Minneapolis: University of Minnesota Press, 1993.

Dreyfus, Hubert L. *What Computers Still Can't Do*. Cambridge, Massachussetts: The MIT Press, 1992.

Eco, Umberto. *Mouse or Rat? Translation as Negotiation*. London: Weidenfeld & Nicolson, 2003.

Flusser, Vilem. *Towards a Philosophy of Photography*. London: Reaktion Books, 2000.

Foucault, Michel. *The Archaeology of Knowledge*. London: Tavistock Publications, 1972.

_____. *The Order of Things*. New York: Vintage Books, 1973.

Freeman, Walter J. *Neurodynamics: An Exploration in Mesoscopic Brain Dynamics*. London: Springer, 2000.

Fynsk, Christopher. *Heidegger: Thought and Historicity*. Ithaca and London: Cornell University Press, 1986.

Gleick, James. *Chaos: Making a New Science*. New York: Penguin Books, 1987.

Hawkins, Jeff. *On Intelligence*. New York: Times Books, 2004.

Heidegger, Martin. *Basic Writings.* London: Routledge, 1993.

_____. *Being and Time.* Oxford: Basil Blackwell, 1962.

_____. *Identity and Difference.* Chicago and London: The University of Chicago Press, 1969.

_____. *Pathmarks.* Cambridge: Cambridge University Press, 1998.

_____. *The Question Concerning Technology and Other Essays.* New York: Harper Torchbooks, 1977.

_____. *What is Called Thinking?* New York: HarperPerennial, 1968.

Jaspers, Karl. *Anaximander, Heraclitus, Parmenides, Plotinus, Lao-Tzu, Nagarjuna.* New York and London: Harvest, 1966.

Kant, Immanuel. *The Critique of Judgement.* Oxford: Oxford University Press, 1952.

_____. *Observations on the Feeling of the Beautiful and Sublime.* Berkley, California: University of California Press, 1960.

Kelly, Owen. *Digital Creativity.* London: Calouste Gulbenkian Foundation, 1996.

Kurzweil, Ray. *The Age of Spiritual Machines.* London: Texere, 2001.

Lacoue-Labarthe, Philippe. *Typography.* Stanford: Stanford Univserity Press, 1989.

Lakoff, George. *Women, Fire, and Dangerous Things: What Categories Reveal about the Mind.* Chicago and London: The University of Chicago Press, 1987.

Lakoff, George and Johnson, Mark. *Metaphors We Live By.* Chicago and London: The University of Chicago Press, 1980.

Levi-Strauss, Claude. *Structural Anthropology 1.* London: Peregrine Books, 1977.

Lyotard, Jean-Francois. *The Inhuman.* Stanford: Stanford University Press, 1991.

_____. *Lessons on the Analytic of the Sublime.* Stanford, California: Stanford University Press, 1994.

Manovich, Lev. *The Language of New Media.* Cambridge, Massachussetts: The MIT Press, 2001.

Miller, Daniel and Slater, Don. *The Internet: An Ethnographic Approach.* Oxford: Berg, 2000.

Moravec, Hans. *Robot: Mere Machine to Transcendent Mind.* Oxford: Oxford University Press, 1999.

Nancy, Jean-Luc. *The Ground of the Image.* New York: Fordham University Press, 2005.

————. *The Muses.* Stanford: Stanford University Press, 1996.

Nietzsche, Friedrich. *The Birth of Tragedy.* New York: Doubleday, 1956.

Ott, Hugo. *Martin Heidegger: A Political Life.* London: Fontana, 1994.

Penrose, Roger. *The Emperor's New Mind.* Oxford: Oxford University Press, 1999.

Pinker, Steven. *The Language Instinct.* London: Penguin, 1994.

Sapir, Edward. *Language.* New York: Harvest Books, 1949.

Schirmacher, Wolfgang (Ed.). *German 20th Century Philosophy: The Frankfurt School.* New York: Continuum, 2000.

Scott, Alwyn. *Stairway to the Mind.* New York: Springer, 1995.

Searle, John R. *The Mystery of Consciousness.* London: Granta Books, 1997.

Sokal, Alan and Bricmont, Jean. *Intellectual Impostures.* London: Profile Books, 1998.

Turkle, Sherry. *Life on the Screen.* New York: Touchstone, 1995.

Ulmer, Gregory. *Applied Grammatology: Post(e)-Pedagogy from Jacques Derrida to Joseph Beuys.* Baltimore and London: The Johns Hopkins University Press, 1985.

————. *Heuretics: The Logic of Invention.* Baltimore and London: The Johns Hopkins University Press, 1994.

————. *Internet Invention: From Literacy to Electracy.* New York: Longman, 2003.

Wittgenstein, Ludwig. *Philosophical Investigations.* Oxford: Blackwell, 2001.

Zielinski, Siegfried. *Audiovisions: Cinema and television as entr'actes in history.* Amsterdam: Amsterdam University Press, 1999.

————. *Deep Time of the Media.* Cambridge, Massachusetts: The MIT Press, 2006.

Zizek, Slavoj. *The Ticklish Subject.* London: Verso, 1999.

CPSIA information can be obtained at www.ICGtesting.com
Printed in the USA
LVOW062323130812

294150LV00001B/170/P